ANIMAL
COMMUNICATION

BOOT CAMP

A step by step guide to help you achieve a deeper
communication with your pets and the animal world.

Debbie McGillivray

Copyright © 2015 Debbie McGillivray

All rights reserved.

ISBN-13: 978-1495922510
ISBN-10: 1495922510

DEDICATION

This book is dedicated to all God's creatures. It is my hope that all humans will be able to see into the souls of the animal world and trust that through love and compassion anything is possible. When we hear the animals, we can help them heal. When we heal the animals, we heal ourselves and the world we live in.

<u>Contents</u>

ACKNOWLEDGEMENTS

A special thank you to Ann Marie Sharp for her dedication to the tedious process of proofing and editing. Without her help, this book would still be sitting in my "To Do" file. Gratitude and love to my family for their love and support throughout this process.

It is my desire for all God's creatures to be acknowledged for their depth of wisdom, love and forgiveness. I have had many remarkable teachers and I am grateful for each and every one of them, both two and four legged. But most of all, to God, for giving us the gift of unconditional love that is often mirrored back to us through our animal's eyes.

1

BOOT CAMP BASICS

Welcome to

ANIMAL COMMUNICATION

BOOT CAMP

Are you looking at your animal wondering... what are you thinking? Do you want to understand your animal on a level deeper than you ever thought possible? If you really want to get in tune with the animal world ... it is time to get busy. Each chapter in this book presents the reader with a no nonsense approach to learning animal communication in an easy to use format. So get off the couch, stop the excuses and let's get started!

Boot Camp Basics

Welcome to the amazing world of telepathic communication with animals. This course is broken down into steps and levels to allow you to develop your abilities at a pace you are comfortable with. Each chapter will have a variety of exercises for you to do and experience in an effort to assist you in developing your telepathic muscle. You will need an open heart, an open mind and a desire to learn. It is also helpful to keep a journal of your progress and communications. I look forward to sharing this journey with you!

But can I do it?

If you are reading this, chances are you believe in telepathic communication with animals and want to learn more. Congratulations, you are past the most difficult part! It takes a lot of courage to come forth and believe in something that many find unbelievable. When I first started, the idea of telepathic communication with animals was not very popular, but thanks to many pioneers in this field the notion of animal communication started to become more mainstream and not so taboo. Now you can find lots of books on the subject and a number of communicators in each state. But still, the vast majority of our society finds this idea either unbelievable or something that only a gifted few can do. The happy ending to this story is that we all possess this ability. If you believe you can do it, then it is possible. I am honored to help you down this path.

How I got started:

My First Teacher - Tyler the Goat

I will never forget my first validated conversation with an animal. It was at Spring Farm Cares Animal Sanctuary. My friends and I drove from Massachusetts to upstate New York to take a weekend animal communication workshop. I was skeptical about this at the time. It all sounded too good to be true and I believed that maybe only a gifted few are born with this ability. I certainly didn't have a psychic bone in my body, so I thought. On the flip side of that, what if by some miraculous intervention I am able to hear the animals? I may become a "basket case" of emotions. I can't even sit through a Disney movie without crying! How will I be able to handle knowing an animal is sad or in pain?

I put my fears aside and decided to keep an open mind. After two full days of exercises it was finally time for the class to go off and attempt to communicate with the animals on the farm. I was excited! I had my pen and paper in hand and marched out to the barn. As I entered the barn I heard a lot of things, but my direction was pulled over to a goat that was perched upon his gate. As I approached him, I heard "Don't ya think I'm handsome?" "Well yeah," I responded. I smirked, thinking I am making this up and when I leave here my husband is going to ship me off to the funny farm for sure. Then I thought I heard the goat comment that my pants were funny. I looked down, what was I thinking wearing blue flowered stretch pants, what a fashion no no. And how embarrassing that my wardrobe was being ridiculed by a goat! This was all very amusing but I thought it surely all has to be my imagination. Then what came next surprised me. I heard "So, what do you think of my ornaments?" Wow, where did that come from? I know I did not make this up. A bit confused, I wrote those exact words down in my notebook. Then I heard "move along, there are others who want to speak to me." "Ok" I said, and thanked him.

When we all returned to class we were supposed to

share what we got from the animals. I finally mustered up the guts to repeat what I heard. The teacher laughed, and stated that the barn staff always tells Tyler that he has nice ornaments, because he always has hay or grass hanging from his horns. My jaw dropped and I knew at that moment that this is real and there was no way I could have made that up. From that day forward I practiced daily with the enthusiasm of a child. I formed practice groups, read every book I could on the subject and began to strengthen my telepathic muscle to the point where I felt I could actually help people with their own animals, and somehow make a difference. I still remember my first client and I still chat with her horse today. I made flyers and posted them at local metaphysical book stores and developed a website. I had a few clients, who referred friends and family to me and that was how my business basically started. I didn't advertise, but relied on word of mouth. I used to wake up in the morning and do my barn chores (at the time I had two horses), then I would squeeze in a few consultations before going to my "normal" nine to five job. Then I would rush home to feed my horses and critters, ride, eat and then sit down to do animal communication sessions in the evening. Eventually it got to the point that something had to give, so I mustered up the courage to quit my job and allowed the animal communication to be my full time occupation. It didn't take long to book up and I felt comfortable in my decision. And as they say, the rest is history.

My life was forever changed. Voices that once fell silent could now be heard and understood. My goal is to help you through this process.

Telepathic Communication

We all communicate through telepathy, yet most of us don't call it this, or don't pay much attention to it. Animals communicate this way regularly which makes it so much easier to communicate with animals via telepathy than people.

Telepathy is the direct transmission of feelings, intentions, thoughts, mental images, emotions, impressions, sensations and pure knowing. Telepathy means "feeling across distance." Telepathic communication can be done in person or over distance. Have you ever thought of someone and the phone rings a minute later and it is them? This is a common example of a telepathic connection. Everything has consciousness and an essence. All live things hold information.

Humans are born with this ability, but as we are socialized we become dependent on verbal communication and our telepathic skills lay hidden. Telepathy is like a muscle, unless used regularly it becomes weak and inefficient. This is why practice is so important.

Humans can carry a lot of "baggage" and personal blocks. Many times we will need to work on breaking down our own walls, preconceived notions and personal "cages" so that we can open up enough to hear the animals.

Telepathy is SUBTLE communication. With practice you will be able to feel confident in the way you receive information from the animals. It is an evolutionary process; you will continually learn and grow. Flex this muscle as often as possible because the more you use it the stronger it will become. Throughout this book you will be presented with various exercises. It is important that you do each exercise with a continued belief that you can do it.

Different ways of receiving information from the animals

Clairvoyance - (Visual) See pictures/scenes

When you connect with an animal, you will see them with your mind's eye. When you ask them a question, you may see subtle pictures. It will feel like your imagination because many times psychic information or telepathic information comes through our imagination. Our imagination holds many references for our psychic connections to draw from and allows us to do things that our mind may not allow. The imagination is a very powerful tool. We will work on this throughout this book.

Example: A client called me about her horse that she felt was stolen. The horse was on trial with a person who showed interest in buying her, but when she went to check on them after the trial period he and the horse were gone. She contacted me to find out if her horse was okay and where they were. When I connected with the horse I asked the horse to show me where she was and she immediately began to send me pictures. I saw with my mind's eye a chain link fence and a shed in the back of the property where she was kept at night along with rusty old farm machinery in the yard and corn fields across the street. My client said that was the place that the man lived, because she went there to drop the horse off originally but when she went back a few weeks later the place was empty, no man, no horse. I connected with the horse again, to see if she was showing me up to date pictures of where she was and I still got the same visions. The lady decided to take another drive out there, despite the feeling that it was a waste of time (it was a two hour drive). She called me a week later to say she found her horse there and was able to safely take her back home.

Clairaudience - (Audio) Hear words and thoughts

When you connect with an animal and ask them a question you may hear words in your head, it will sound like your own thoughts and words. Your logical mind will immediately write it off as your imagination, but actually this is how the information will come across. You MUST trust it. In trusting you allow more information to come through.

Example: I was in my barn cleaning stalls and one of

my horses came in the barn and was just watching me from his stall. He didn't normally do this when his buddy was outside. Then I heard in my head, "Don't you think it's time you took that sign down?" I looked up, kind of shocked that this thought just "popped" into my head and my horse, Maxx, was just staring at me. I looked at the wall directly across from his stall and there was the sign my husband made me a year prior to us getting Maxx and in big letters it read, "Finnegan's Home." I never thought much about it before, but I guess Maxx was offended, especially when anyone read that sign out loud. Finnegan is my other horse, who we actually built the barn for. I laughed and told Maxx I would remove the sign because it is his home as well. As soon as I took the sign down, Maxx happily left the barn and went about his business.

Kinesthetic - Feel pain or emotions

When you connect with an animal you may feel pain in certain areas of your body that correspond with the animal or you may feel strong emotions.

Example: I had a client call me about her stallion. He had become dangerously aggressive and they were considering putting him down at the urge of the trainer and the state. When I connected with him, I did not get a mean spirited animal, he was quite gentle in the way he communicated. He started showing me that he had immense pain and was mistreated and feared by people. He showed me scenes of people pushing him to the back of his stall with wooden sticks and once he was hit over the head with one. When I asked to scan his body he allowed me to and immediately I began to feel stabbing pain in my head, he then showed me that when he got these headaches it was like a wall of black that came over him and he couldn't see. When this happened he became frightened and lashed out at whatever was around. His blinding headaches sent him into panic mode. While I was connected with him, I too felt the headaches, but on a much more subtle level than what he actually felt. After I disconnected with him, the headache went away.

This poor horse suffered much abuse at the hands of the trainer. The owner took my advice and got the horse out of the trainer's barn and back home to her breeding farm, where she immediately enlisted the help of a chiropractor to work on him (his body was badly out of alignment including his head which contributed to his headaches). His attitude changed completely and she sent me an email saying that this stallion who was once so aggressive is safe enough to allow her daughter to work with him, and since he has come home, has gone on to sire many foals.

Clairsentience - A general "knowing"

Sometimes when we connect with an animal and ask a question, we may feel like we are not getting any of the above, but you may just have a general knowing. For example, you may just know that this animal misses its' previous owner or wants to have a baby or needs to retire, etc. Trust this general knowing or gut feeling. A lot of times we experience this more with our own animals.

Example: I went to the barn one day to see my horse, Finnegan. I knew the minute I saw his face that something was wrong. I couldn't explain it, there was no physical sign at the time, but I just had a gut feeling. An hour later he started to colic. (Colic is similar to a stomach ache in people, but is very painful and can be caused by gas or impaction in horses.)   Usually veterinary care is needed. I trusted my gut and took the necessary steps to help him.

Tasting

Sometimes information will come through as a taste in your mouth.

Example: I had a client who asked me what her horse's favorite treat was and I tasted peppermint in my mouth. Sure enough, his favorite treats were peppermints. Pay attention to any information you are getting, it comes in all forms.

Smelling

Sometimes information will come through as a scent.

Example: I had a client whose dog was very ill all of a sudden. When we connected with the dog to ask him what was making him sick, all I could smell was bleach. The person confirmed that she had recently cleaned the floors with bleach in the kitchen where the dog ate. The dog was a messy eater and would often drop his food on the floor to eat it. He must have inadvertently ingested some of the bleach residue.

Examples of how different people may receive information from their pets:

If you ask a dog what his favorite thing to do is you may:

- See a still picture of a ball

- See a scene in your mind's eye of the dog jumping in the air and catching a ball

- Hear the word ball

- Feel the exhilaration of running and catching a ball in your teeth

If you ask a dog how his body feels you may:

- Hear "My stomach hurts"

- Feel your stomach twitching or moving

- See a picture of a stomach

- See the scene of the dog going over to the neighbor's house and eating the dog treats they give him then getting sick

- Sensing/Knowing – Just knowing that his stomach hurts

When I first started, I mostly got information as words. I did a lot of automatic writing when I was practicing my communication technique. As my telepathic muscle expanded and became stronger I began to get more pictures both moving and still, then feelings in my body, then words, etc. I also found that the way in which I worked with animals sometimes changed how I received information. For instance, when I worked with clients and their animals over the phone, the information usually streamed in primarily as pictures first, then words and feelings. When I worked with live animals and sat with a notebook and pen, the information streamed through more as words followed by pictures. Allow the information to flow through you, don't try to control or judge it.

You may receive information in a variety of ways; just remember to accept what you get. By doing this you allow more information to come through. Doubt is natural, but it is very important to put it aside during this process. If you doubt yourself too much while connecting with an animal, it may offend the animal or cause them to back off in their communication with you.

Building Blocks for Success

Just like any good program, you have to start with the basics and from there you will create a good foundation from which you will grow. Without the proper foundation you may find yourself creating blocks that will sabotage your communication abilities. Being present in the moment allows our mind to be in the here and now. We are a multi-tasking society. I am guilty of this as well. To sit still and just be present, fully present, without checking our phones, emails, thinking about the past or future, can be a challenge and almost seem like a frivolous waste of valuable time. But this is one luxury we must try to incorporate into our lives daily. Trust me; it will pay off in more ways than one. Not only will you be more receptive to all intuitive information, you will also become more effective in all of your activities.

The first step of this communication boot camp is to develop this skill and come to realize the importance of it. Being present in the moment simply means directing your full attention to your surroundings at that time and acknowledging things that go unnoticed when we go through life "unaware." It is making a conscious effort to not think about what you have to do later, or what you didn't accomplish yesterday, but a rare opportunity for you to observe the here and now, relishing in the gift of the present moment.

The challenge of telepathic communication is not doing it, we are doing it all the time without realizing it, the challenge is to access it with full awareness and attention. Being in the moment is a hard thing to do for any length of time with our busy lives.

Exercise:

Sit outside and allow yourself to just be present in that very moment. Listen to all the sounds that would otherwise have gone unnoticed. Allow yourself to really see and look at everything around you. Use your nose to smell all the lovely scents that nature has to offer. Enjoy being fully present in that moment, and allow yourself to be grateful for this.

Try to do this exercise in different locations, to get yourself used to being fully present.

Exercise:

Have you ever noticed that sometimes when you are having a conversation with someone, you may only be half listening? Your mind may be thinking about lots of other things as you nod your head acknowledging what the person you are talking with is saying, even though you are not fully engaged in the conversation. We are a multi-tasking society, which is both good and bad at times. This next exercise may sound simple but for some may be very difficult. Next time you are having a conversation with someone, either in person or on the phone, try to be fully present. That means listening to the person, not interrupting or letting your mind wander off. Try to remain fully present throughout the whole conversation. If you are talking to someone in person make sure your body reflects being present as well. Sitting quietly and looking at the person while you listen. If you are talking on the phone make sure you are not trying to do other tasks, which is a habit all of us are guilty of. For the purpose of this exercise, it is important that you remain fully engaged in the conversation. The person you are speaking with may even thank you for it! You may wonder why this exercise is necessary when doing telepathic communication. It is imperative for you to be present in the moment to achieve as pure a connection as possible.

Grounding your energy

When you ground your energy, you become more balanced energetically. If you can imagine what a flame looks like jumping all around, or a sparkler sputtering sparks in every direction, this is what our energy may look like to an animal if we are ungrounded, nervous, stressed, hyper or spacey. When we ground our energy we balance it so that it appears more calm and controlled. Animals trust this energy much more than an ungrounded energy. You can also become ungrounded if you do a lot of psychic activity, or come out of a meditation or dream state where you have not properly anchored your energy. Have you ever woken from a dream very groggy and confused? Chances are your energy was still "out there" somewhere and did not have a chance to anchor itself back to the earth. Sounds silly, but once you begin to experience the difference you will understand how vital it can be.

There are many different ways to ground your energy and the more you begin to work with telepathy and intuition, the more you will need to "ground" your energy. Examples of not being "grounded" are the feeling of being lightheaded or spacey. If you are working with animals that may have an emotional or physical trauma that you pick up, you may inadvertently carry that emotional or physical feeling with you after you have disconnected from the animal. If this happens you will need to ground and protect your energy. I will go over the different ways of doing this.

Exercise:

Grounding your energy

Sit comfortably in a chair or on the ground. If in a chair, make sure your feet are touching the ground. You can also do this exercise standing up if you wish.

Imagine roots growing out of your feet into the earth below. Imagine the energy of the earth coming up through your feet and out the top of your head. Feel your body becoming more balanced, your mind becoming relaxed and your spirit more in sync with the body and mind.

Another effective way to ground yourself is by going outside and actually touching the earth and feeling the dirt between your fingers. Allow yourself to just be present while doing this, try not to let your mind take over. Tune into the world around you and the feeling of the earth under your feet. Stand up and "feel" your energy being centered in your body.

Those tree huggers knew what they were doing! Hugging a tree will immediately ground you to the earth. It is about being connected once again with the rhythms of nature and the earth. Just walking out in nature will bring you to this state if you let it. Why do people flock to the ocean? Not just to work on their tan, but unknown to many, the ocean heals. When we walk barefoot we are absorbing the frequencies of the earth and it grounds and relaxes us. So go ahead, take your shoes off and enjoy the feel of the sand, the ocean or the green grass under your feet. Play like a child again and feel the pulsing energies that are all around you. I give you permission to play!

Protecting your energy

If you feel like you are carrying a heavy emotional or physical weight around that may not be yours, you may want to cleanse and protect your energy field. Have you ever chatted with a person who drained you of your energy and left you in a bad mood or perhaps a depressed state? Or have you ever walked into a building and immediately sensed something bad, or felt physically ill? Sometimes unwanted energy will cling to us and weigh us down. By cleansing and protecting your energy, much like washing our hands, it frees us of unwanted emotions or feelings that are not ours.

There are many different ways of doing this. I will list a few, try each one to see which one fits you the best at this time.

Exercise:

- Imagine an illuminating white light swirling around

your body (like a cocoon) and protecting you from any unwanted energy attachment from another being. As this white light swirls around your body, allow it to gently cleanse your energy field with its loving white light.

- Imagine breathing in the white illuminating light with twinkles of purple and gold. As you breathe in deep, allow this white light to cleanse your energy of anything that is not yours. Imagine this white light infusing through your body and as you exhale, release anything that needs to be removed. Allow that energy to gently disperse into the universe. Take a few deep breaths until you feel you are cleansed and protected.

- Imagine yourself as a mighty oak tree with large branches sprouting out the top of you and cascading down your energy field as white light, gently protecting your energy field.

Sacred Silence

Sacred silence or meditation is simply a bridge from our physical consciousness to our spiritual consciousness, and it is here that we have access to truth. We get out of our head/mind and focus more on the spirit and heart connection. It is in this state that we can access information, healing energy and much more.

Many people become intimidated by the word meditation. I too have balked at this idea for years. Think of it as simply calming the mind and experiencing silence by slowing the mind down so that your body and mind become relaxed. It allows tension to fade and gives relaxation a chance to filter in. It allows the mind, body and spirit to become more in balance and aligned. There are many different types of meditation or calming of the mind including breathing exercises. We will explore many of these.

Mind Calming Exercises:

Take three cleansing breaths – breathe deeply through the nose, hold for the count of two, then release through the mouth. Take one breath to cleanse the body, one breath to calm the mind, and the third breath to open the heart. Imagine yourself sitting on a large flat rock at the edge of a beautiful lake. The sky is perfectly blue, there is a slight breeze and the sun feels warm on your skin. You can hear the birds happily chirping and the sound of the water lapping against the shore. You can smell the earth and water. As you sit on this rock, allow yourself to be still like the water before you, crystal clear and still. Look out over the water and allow yourself to become tranquil by its beauty. As the water gently laps against the shore, you relax fully into the grace before you. Stay here for as long as you like. When you are ready to return, step off the rock onto the ground and allow the energy of the earth to flow up through your feet and out the top of your head. Feel centered and grounded in your body.

Water or Nature

Simply soaking in a tub or floating in a pool or ocean can put your mind and body at ease immediately. For others just sitting outside in nature connects us to the sacred silence in our mind we hunger for during our busy lives.

Tracing a symbol with your mind's eye

Begin by closing your eyes. Take a deep breath in through your nostrils and hold for the count of three and exhale through your mouth. As you inhale, allow the air to fill up your lungs and diaphragm, and feel your chest rise up. As you exhale, feel the air release at first in the throat, chest and then diaphragm. Feel any tension leave your body. Inhale again and hold for the count of three, then exhale fully through your mouth. Feel centered in your body. Now simply focus your attention on the infinity sign in your mind's eye. Allow your mind to follow the lines of this symbol as if you were searching for the end. You can also do this with a circle if you like. Allow yourself to do this for as long as you can stay focused.

Conscious Breathing

Sit or lie down in a relaxing spot, free from distractions. It may be helpful to have new age or meditation music playing in the background (I love the *I AM Wishes Fulfilled Meditation* music by Dr. Wayne Dyer and James Twyman). Focus on your breathing; allow your stomach to rise and fall with each breath. Do this for approximately one minute. With the next deep breath feel it fill your stomach and then rise up into your chest and then to the top of your throat. Hold this breath for the count of three and then exhale through your mouth. Do this again and this time as you exhale release any tension, doubt or distractions from your body. Do this for three to five breaths and fully believe that you are releasing any tension out of the body. You can also think of the words IN for the inhale, and OUT for the exhale. You can say them in your mind which will add focus and help you to further still the mind.

Continue to do this type of breathing for 10 minutes a few times a day. If thoughts pop into your mind, just acknowledge them, and then release them. Continue to stay in this "no mind" of peace and relaxation. If you feel parts of your body that are tense, gently allow the tension to be exhaled out. Allow yourself to feel fully centered and relaxed in your body. When you feel it is time to come back you can begin to wiggle each body part. Take in a deep breath and imagine roots growing out of your feet deep into the earth below. Feel the energy of the earth come up through the roots, into your feet and out the top of your head. When you are ready, you can slowly open your eyes. (Don't jump up too quickly or you may feel lightheaded.)

Entering Still Point

There is a still moment between an exhale and the next inhale. This is called still point. Focus on this short period of time, and work on slowing your breath so that you can remain in still point for longer periods of time. Please work on this each night at bedtime. It will be wonderfully relaxing to your body and mind. For years I had trouble sleeping, and when I began my meditation practice my sleep was drastically improved. If I did wake up in the middle of the night and had trouble going back to sleep, I would do my "so-hum" breathing and "still point" and I would drift peacefully back to sleep without my mind hijacking my body with its rogue thoughts of worry, fear and doubt.

Understanding the energy and essence in all things

All things have energy. Energy is something that never dies, it just shifts and changes. Trees are alive; they have energy and access to knowledge from higher planes. Yes, we can communicate with trees, plants, flowers, insects, fish, etc.

You may already know this, or you may be thinking that this is just a little bit far fetched. Trust me, you can communicate with all living things. The Native Americans knew the significance of this and honored this process. We have the knowledge imbedded in our cells, we just need to let our modern day mind and doubts be still enough for us to tune in to this new world. If you allow yourself to do this, you will witness miracles on many levels. The world is not as it seems. By tapping into this whole process, you have allowed yourself the privilege of being one with all life. This is not something that happens overnight, it is a process of understanding and accepting. In honoring all living things, we allow our spirit and those around us to blossom.

The logical mind will always try to dominate the intuition. However, by meditating, we are in fact singing a lullaby to the logical mind so that it naps for a bit. This is when the intuition starts to come to life.

Sending and Receiving Information

The importance of sending information to an animal is often overlooked. By being present in the moment and clear in your messages, you increase your accuracy that the animal will understand and that you will receive information clearly. By setting your intention to connect with a certain animal, you are setting up a direct transmission to that animal just like a radio. If you have a poor connection, there may be a lot of static to pick through. If our mind is full of other thoughts when we connect with an animal, the connection will not be as pure as it could be. Keep things simple and clear in the beginning.

We must realize that when we "talk" to an animal we are sending more things than we actually realize. When we verbally talk to an animal, they are picking up our mental thoughts and pictures that lay hidden behind the words, as well as emotions and tone. When we communicate telepathically the same is true. We can have a "tone" when we communicate telepathically as well. Telepathic communication is much more efficient than verbal communication; it is immediate and not as cumbersome as verbal. All communication is an interpretation on both sides. We must put aside our own preconceived notions and fears when communicating with an animal.

When communicating something to an animal, it is important to send the information as clear as possible. A few things to remember are:

- Setting your intention to clearly communicate with "said" animal.

- Being quiet in your mind or present in the moment. Try not to let your mind wander or drift while you are communicating something to an animal.

- Keep your pictures and words crisp and clear. When you are picturing something for an animal, create the scene as realistic as possible. Example: When I work with clients who are concerned that their cat or dog is going too close to the street, I always explain to the animal the dangers of the street, and also picture for them what can happen to them as vividly as possible. I go so far as to show them how sad their person would be if they got hit by a car or hurt in anyway. I picture this and send them the emotion as well. I also picture for them very graphically what can happen to them if they got hit by a car and how quickly it can happen even if they are very careful.

One of the most important tips I can give you is this; **animals want to know "what to do," _not_ "what not to do." Animals like to know what they can do... give them a job or purpose ... instead of always saying no. This builds self esteem, responsibility, and a sense of purpose.**

Because animals often read the pictures behind our words, by telling an animal what we want them to do we send a picture of exactly that.

For instance: Chloe, a lab cross, loved to chew on her person's furniture when she went to work. As a result, Chloe got in big trouble and eventually was crated or locked in the kitchen while her person went to work. I asked Laura, Chloe's person, what she told her dog before she left for work and she told her everyday not to chew the sofa. I asked her to say that slowly and pay attention to what she is picturing when she says this. She was silent on the other end and then said, well I know what I am saying but I guess I am picturing her chewing the sofa. I told her that many times it is the pictures behind the words that the animals pay attention to. I told her that we needed to give her dog a job to do while she was away at work and explain to her the rules of the home. I told her to ask Chloe to watch over the house and keep everything in order – this way she was picturing her walking around the house, leaving things alone, and doing a good job so that her person would reward her when she came home. It gave Chloe's excess energy a focus, made her feel important and gave her something to think about besides chewing the sofa. And the best part, her reward was an energetic play session outside that allowed her to alleviate any built up tension or energy she gathered throughout the day.

Exercise:

Color exercise – sending and receiving. For this exercise you will need to get another willing participant to help you. It is important that the person be as open to this as possible.

1) Sit across from each other, either in chairs, couch or floor. Wherever you are most comfortable but can face one another. Explain to your partner that this is a sending and receiving game. You will take turns picking a color and sending the color to your partner. One person will be the sender the other the receiver, then you will switch.

2 The sender should take a minute silently to think about what color they will choose, pick an object that is that color as well as if it is a warm or cool color. (For instance you may pick the color orange, picking

the orange fruit to send to your partner, sending a cool refreshing feeling along with it, saying the word orange in your mind and you may even imagine what that fresh orange may smell like). When the sender is ready to send, they will verbally let the receiver know they are sending the color telepathically to them. When sending – imagine sending the color like a ray of light from their forehead to the receiver's forehead. You can even picture the object for your partner but continue to send it directly to your partner's third eye or forehead. The receiver's job is to just close their eyes and try to "get" what picture the sender is sending. Send for approximately 20 seconds and then stop and tell receiver to open their eyes.

3) Prior to beginning the exercise, you may want to guide your partner in three to five deep breaths to clear the mind. It does not matter right now if you get it right or wrong. What you are getting is the feel for sending information clearly. Your logical mind

will try to butt in, just politely ask it to take the back seat while your spiritual mind plays. The more you do this exercise the better you will become. For now, do not get hung up on getting it right or you will cloud your receiving ability with this notion. "Getting it right" is the logical mind intruding. The spiritual mind simply receives without judgment and accepts what it gets. This exercise is more about the clarity of sending rather than getting the color right.

2

THE COMMUNICATION SIX PACK

These are the basic steps in preparing you for a telepathic communication with an animal.

The Communication Six Pack

Breathe

Open your heart

State your intention

Greetings

Tune in

Gratitude

Breathe: Take three deep cleansing breaths to center

your energy, slow your mind, and relax the body.

Open your heart: Telepathic communication with an animal is really a heart to heart communication or exchange. Our hearts may be closed for many reasons: fear of pain...both emotional and physical, present and past, a fear that you can't do this, apprehension about hearing an animal's pain, fear, or unhappiness, etc. Opening your heart happens in a variety of ways. During my workshops some people will break down into tears and may have no idea what triggered it. Others will have connected with one of my animal teachers who moved their soul. This is an opening of your heart big and wide. If this happens to you, don't worry it was meant to. When I took my first animal communication class, I walked into the barn to begin communicating and approached one horse that moved me to tears. He didn't say much, but I felt in my heart what he felt. I instruct my students to picture a door on their heart. You can make this door look like anything you want; a glass door, a big heavy wooden door, a colorful door, etc. Then prior to each connection imagine opening this door wide. After a while you won't need to do this step as it will happen naturally. But for now, it is important to imagine this door open when you connect with an animal.

State your intention: This is another important step that is downplayed in many books or classes on animal communication. It is important to state your intention, especially when working with animals long distance. This sets up the connection to the exact animal you wish to connect with. There will be times that other animals in the home will try to come through first, but usually it is because the animal you intended to connect with allowed it. Stating your intention will sound something like this:

Standard Intention: "My intention is to speak with (animal's name)." Then you would call the animal's name in your head a few times to create the connection and get the animal's attention.

Long Distance Intention: When connecting to an animal that is not in front of you:

"My intention is to speak with (animal's name), located in (town/state), whose person is (person's first name)." Then you would call the animal's name in your head a few times to create the connection and get the animal's attention. After connecting with the animal, I like to picture them in my mind's eye using the physical description the owner provided.

Greetings: Be sure to introduce yourself to the animal and say hello. Then you may ask permission to speak with them. In the beginning, this will be the start of your dialogue or communication. In the learning phase, it is important that you start by imagining the animal saying hi back to you. I also like to admire something about the animal (oh what a silky coat you have, etc.). They are very receptive to this.

Tune in: Be still in your mind and allow the essence of the animal to filter through.

Ask questions and tune in to the animal. If you do not get anything, ask the question again or ask another question.

Gratitude: Thank the animal for opening up and speaking to you. Gratitude creates an environment of trust and respect.

TIPS - to help you communicate with the animals:

Attitude - The way you view animals will influence your communication receptivity and the willingness of the animals you are connecting with. Approach animals with respect and appreciation for who they are. If you view them as substandard or inferior in any way you will limit your ability and awareness. In order to truly experience the spiritual essence of each being, you will need to leave any preconceived notions and fears behind. Open your heart and allow the animal's true being to come through to you. Be humble and receptive and the animal will feel comfortable in opening up to you. Admiring the animal's spiritual qualities such as their honesty, loyalty, patience, joy, integrity, wisdom, kindness, etc., will help to encourage mutual respect and build the relationship into one of deeper understanding ultimately strengthening the two-way communication between both of you. View each being as an individual, with respect and love and see them as a potential teacher. This will enable you to observe them with objectivity, allowing the information to flow into you.

Quiet your mind – This can be a challenge in today's world. Take time out daily to quiet your mind. Try sitting quietly with your animals and just "being" present with them. You can also try yoga, meditation, soothing music, exercise, etc., anything that will help quiet the cluttering thoughts that create traffic in your head.

If you find that you are still having a hard time quieting your mind, you can also try changing your diet, spending more time in nature and meditating daily. See what works for you. What may work for someone else may not necessarily work for you. Experiment with the different ways of relaxing your mind.

Open your heart – Imagine that there are two big doors that lead to your heart. Inhale deeply, hold for the count of two and exhale. As you open the doors to your heart, inhale deeply; one, two, and exhale through your mouth.

Feel the tension melt away – feel the love consume you – center yourself in your body and deeply inhale/exhale.

Believe in yourself – Believe in your intuitive ability. This will be the hardest step for some. Accept whatever you get and thank the animal. Pay attention to everything you feel, see, hear and smell. Don't discount anything. In order to remove the blocks for successful two-way communication, you must believe it is possible and believe in your intuition. I guarantee that each one of you will say, "It feels like I am talking to myself." This is what it feels like in the beginning. As you practice more and trust what you receive, you will develop more confidence in yourself.

Be receptive – Be open to anything you get. It may test your conventional notions, accept it and acknowledge the animal for it. If you are not clear what you are receiving, ask again. Be open to surprises. Shut off your mind – there is no room for logic here. Just accept anything you get, no matter how strange it may be.

Don't overwhelm –Be careful not to project your own strong emotions towards the animal. If you are putting out strong emotions, whether it is love, fear, or sadness, you could block the two-way process or only get back your own emotions.

Don't try too hard – This is a common mistake in the

beginning. If you try too hard you will miss the subtle communication that is taking place. It is very subtle. Shift into the receptive mode – lean back, open chest and hands, breathe slowly and deeply, close your eyes if you like, relax and let it flow.

Accept - Pay attention to everything you receive; whether it is feelings, pictures, impressions, thoughts, words, sounds, bodily sensations, or just a knowing. Become familiar with what and how you receive information. Don't analyze or criticize. Remain non-judgmental. Do not be afraid to acknowledge what you get, this will open up intuitive doors for you in many ways. Do not worry about what others may think for this will only set up blocks for you. Accept and acknowledge what you receive and let the meaning or story unfold by itself. It will be different for everyone, so do not compare yourself to others, accept what you get. The more you doubt yourself, the more you will inhibit the flow.

<u>Practice</u> – The key to building the telepathic muscle is practice.

<u>Have fun</u> – Keep it lighthearted and fun. Don't get frustrated. If you feel you are not receiving anything, review the previous steps again. We all have bad days and many things can inhibit telepathy. Remember to have fun.

<u>Gratitude</u> – Always acknowledge what you receive from the animal and thank them. This keeps them receptive to you and willing to continue.

Imagination Communication

Exercise:

Take a moment to find a quiet place to sit, inside or outside. Take a few deep breaths, one to clear the body, one to quiet the mind, and one to light the spirit. Smile and allow all tension to drain from your body. Take three more deep breaths to relax even more.

Now, pick any animal you know that pops into your head as your teacher for this exercise. Imagine they are standing in front of you. Really see all the details of them; eyes, mouth, ears, nose, fur/coat, tail, feet, etc. Next, imagine you say hello and they respond back. Ask them to tell you something about themselves. "Imagine" they tell you something back. Ask them anything you wish, have an imaginary conversation with this being. And when done, thank this animal for helping you. Write down whatever you get.

Exercising Your Inner Eye and Senses:

Taking your time, translate each of the following

descriptions into a mental image. Go back and do it again in a few weeks and then a few weeks later, and notice the difference.

Now sense (see, touch, hear, taste, and smell) with your mind's eye:

> ➤ The face of your animal friend
> ➤ A horse running through the snow
> ➤ The waves crashing on the beach
> ➤ Your favorite spot
> ➤ Drawing a figure eight on a piece of paper
> ➤ The sound of thunder
> ➤ The voice of a friend
> ➤ Dogs barking
> ➤ An itch
> ➤ A gentle breeze on your face
> ➤ Walking up hill
> ➤ A bell ringing
> ➤ The feeling of hunger
> ➤ The feeling of an ice cube on your

forehead

- ➢ The feeling of a sore knee
- ➢ The feeling of a toothache
- ➢ The taste of a lemon
- ➢ The taste of chocolate
- ➢ The taste of a potato chip
- ➢ The smell of fresh cut grass
- ➢ The smell of bread baking
- ➢ The smell of the earth

In the Animal's Skin:

This is a great exercise to help you feel what it's like to be in an animal's body. Refer back to this process when you are working with lost animals or doing body scans.

Imagine yourself as an animal with every cell of your being. You can use an animal card deck if you like, a picture from a magazine, or just randomly pick any animal that pops into your mind for this exercise. Be sure to read this exercise in full before you start so that you can do it without stopping to read, or have a friend guide you through it.

- Pick out a picture of an animal, fish, insect, bird or reptile.

- Take three deep breaths.

- Imagine yourself looking at this animal right in front of you. Then imagine your energy morphing or overlapping into the body of this animal. You are now in the body of this animal. You are looking out the eyes of this animal now.

- Take a moment to let the energy become real.

- Feel their body; what does it feel like to be in this body. How does your skin or hair feel, your head – mouth, teeth, jaw, nose, eyes, ears......

- Move down your neck and into your back.....down

each leg and into the feet. If you have wings or fins, experience what they feel like on each side of your body. Work your way towards the back of the body and feel the rump and tail.

- Feel yourself moving as this being. How does your body feel?

- What type of terrain is under your feet and what is the climate?

- How do you see, hear, smell, taste, and touch?

- What do you eat?

- Where do you rest or sleep?

- What do you like to do during the day?

- Do you have a name and are you male or female?

- Are you alone or with others?

- Are you young or old?

- What do you fear?

- What do you love to do?

- Describe yourself in one word.

- Exit the body, ground yourself, and thank the animal.

(When you exit the body, imagine once again that you are looking at the animal in front of you. Thank the animal for letting you experience this and ground your energy).

Can you hear me now?

Making the Connection

When connecting with an animal in person, you will be going through all the steps as explained in the previous lessons. The difference in communicating with an animal in person and an animal long distance is that when you are with the animal in person it is important that your body language and energy be as calm and diffused as possible. You can do this by taking a few deep breaths and grounding your energy. This will calm the energy we project out from our body that animals can read and pick up on. We all project a certain energy depending on the situation. By taking a minute to tune in to the energy you are projecting you can change it just by willing it. For instance, if you have a really bad day at work and you come home very upset, your animals will pick up on that immediately. By taking a few cleansing breaths prior to entering the house and thinking about something that makes you smile or happy (picture your energy shifting to a softer color), you can change what you project to others. By doing this you are also attracting that same energy to yourself. You can turn a bad day into a good day with this simple exercise.

Connecting with animals long distance - Setting your intention

When I first started doing this, I worked mostly from pictures and typed out all the information I got from the animals. I got a lot of words and feelings. Then I emailed or called the person back to tell them what I got. As my abilities grew and shifted, I preferred to work without a picture and got images from the animals, then words. I also shifted to working with the person and animal together on the phone. It is important to try different ways of connecting with the animals. You may find that you prefer one method over the other. But remember not to limit yourself. Experience each way of connecting so that your abilities will grow stronger in all areas.

Animal Teacher Exercises:

You will need to work with an animal you do not know too much about so that you can practice connecting and enhancing this skill. If you work with an animal you know too much about in the beginning, your logical mind will make excuses for the intuition and cloud the purity of the connection. Ask a friend or relative if you can work with one of their animals. You can work with them in person or long distance using a picture or by getting a physical description of them and their location.

Receiving the essence of the animal

Once you have your animal teacher, set aside time where you will not be interrupted to do this exercise. If the weather permits, sit outside so that your energy will naturally become grounded to the earth. Take a moment to breathe and relax and then begin the process of connecting to this animal. In your mind explain to this animal teacher that you want to understand their personality better. Ask this animal to show you what they are like. You can connect with them while looking at the picture, or look at the picture then put it down and tune in. I like to picture the animal appearing in the room with me, and then I watch their body language in my mind's eye to give me an idea of what they are trying to tell me or what their personality is like.

After you are connected with this animal's energy, take a moment to answer the following questions:

How do they appear to you? What pictures do you get? What words pop into your head? What emotions are you feeling? Make sure you write down whatever you get. This will allow the information to flow better. When we don't let the information out, either by speaking it or writing it down, it will inhibit the flow.

Ask this animal to describe themselves to you in a few words. (Write down whatever you get.)

What qualities do you see/feel? Some of these may stand out more than others so circle whichever quality best describes your animal teacher's personality and essence.

Are they.........

Dominant – or - Submissive

Confident – or - Cautious

Serious - or - Funny

Affectionate - or - Aloof

Nervous – or - Content

Athletic - or - Sedentary

Sloppy – or - Tidy

Easy going - or - Uptight with change

Friendly - or -Unfriendly

Finicky - or - Eats Anything

Loves attention – or - Prefers to be alone

Plays by the rules – or - Likes testing the rules

Easily frightened – or -Very brave

Playful – or - reserved

Loves everyone - or – Loyal to one

Dominant – or - Submissive

Longtime Resident - or - Newbie

You may connect with your animal teacher as many times as you like. Be sure to thank your animal teacher when you are done.

Exercise:

Pick an animal teacher to work with and set aside time where you will not be interrupted. Remember to go through the connection process of breathing, grounding your energy, opening your heart, stating your intention, and calling the animal's name in your head. Introduce yourself and ask permission to speak to them and, finally, tune in and remember to thank the animal at the end.

Worksheet A

Animal's name:

1) What are your likes/dislikes?

2) Can you tell me about your past?

3) Do you have any fears, if so what?

4) What is your job or purpose?

5) Who are your friends?

6) Where do you like to rest or sleep?

7) Who is your favorite person in the home?

8) What would you like changed?

9) How does your body feel?

10) What do you like to eat?

3

HANDLING COMMON BEHAVIORAL ISSUES

Let's face it, none of us are perfect and many animals come to us with issues that we need to help them work through. It is not always an easy process and sometimes animals are reflecting back to us the very thing that we need to work on ourselves. Some animals come to us with the effects of past trauma and abuse that need to be addressed with compassion and patience; other animals present problems to us so that we may seek out help and/or knowledge to one day help others or help us to find our path. Whatever the reason, there are some great ways in which you can help the animal resolve them. In all instances, people must take an inventory of the energy they inadvertently project and know that they may need to make adjustments as necessary.

Separation Anxiety

Separation anxiety is any type of anxiety associated with being left alone. I see this mostly with dogs and horses, but some cats become highly stressed when their person leaves the home. When animals become stressed, their body becomes susceptible to secondary health concerns. You may notice that when you come back from vacation, all of a sudden your animal is peeing inappropriately or has an upset stomach, etc. Stress has a quick and negative effect on animals and can disrupt the vulnerable areas of their bodies, such as urinary and digestive health. There are certain things you can do to alleviate this type of anxiety.

Understand their fears. It is easy to think a fear is unjustified or unrealistic and you may want to convey to the animal that they have no reason to be afraid. However, without actually acknowledging their fear and empathizing with them, the animal does not trust that you truly understand the scope of fear they are encountering. After you acknowledge what they are going through, it is vital that you shift your energy out of compassion mode and into a leader role. This gives the animal immediate trust in your decisions. Think about it... If you had a fear of flying would you trust the person who was confident and assertive to fly the plane, or would you trust the person who was apologizing for your fear and more concentrated on consoling you? Think about how different these energies are. This is what animals interpret; it is all about the energy we are projecting. We can be compassionate and empathize, but in order for the animal to begin to move forward and trust us to get them through it we must prove that we have the energy and confidence to do so. Here are some ideas about how you can help an animal who has separation anxiety:

- Tell them where you are going, why, and for how long you will be away.

- Give the animal a purpose or job while you are gone, i.e., to watch over house, keep the house neat and clean, patrol the yard, etc.

- Never use "don't" in your visualizations or jobs. Visualize how you would like them to behave in a positive way. Refrain from saying, don't chew the table, etc., because when you say things this way you are actually picturing the bad behavior and unknowingly reinforcing it.

- Shift your energy so that you remove worry and anticipation with a vision of confidence and the behavior you want from the animal.

- Have Rescue Remedy on hand.

Going to the bathroom indoors:

Many people assume that if an animal squats down in front of them and pees inappropriately that they are unhappy with us and letting us know. Sometimes that is the case, but many times it is because they want us to know that something is wrong with their body and they need help. Rule out any health issues first. Common emotional reasons animals may go to the bathroom inside may be:

- Litter box is not clean enough.

- Too many animals for one box.

- Cat Litter hurts feet or burns eyes. Switching to a different litter without perfume and a softer texture can help this. Many cats that have been declawed suffer nerve pain and foot sensitivity as a result and can't stand the feeling of the litter in their toes.

- The animal may associate the cat box or litter with painful urination or constipation from a past or present illness.

- A cat may feel vulnerable using the box,

especially if there is another cat in the home that stalks or dominates them, or if the litter box is in an area that feels unsafe to them.

- Covering up the scent of another animal that may be marking.

- Feeling threatened by feral or wild animals outside the home, or inside the home, i.e., marking territory.

- Too cold or wet outside!

- Anger, lack of boundaries, no understanding of the rules due to a traumatic or neglectful past, and trying to get your attention are also all common reasons for inappropriate bathroom activity.

Common Health reasons that a dog or cat may go to the bathroom in inappropriate areas are:

- Urinary tract infection.

- Bladder stones (very serious in male cats as this can cause blockage and requires an emergency visit to the vet's office. If your cat is squatting before you trying to urinate and nothing is coming out, please seek medical attention immediately).

- Diabetes or Thyroid disorders.

- Parasites or a virus causing them to have an urgency to defecate without warning.

- New medications.

- Painful back or hips when squatting or using stairs can make an animal reluctant to go outside.

Once the root cause is identified you can take steps to resolve the problem either through holistic veterinary care, or in the case of an emotional issue, understanding why the behavior is happening and making a compromise together to correct it. For example: I had a client call me about their cat who starting peeing outside of the litter box. This was happening more and more and ruining their hardwood floors. When I connected with Echo and asked him why he was peeing on the floor, he showed me a big black cat that he saw out the window every day. He said he was very upset that this cat was in his territory and he wanted to make sure that this cat knew this was his house. Echo's person said that she feeds a black feral cat off the back porch and that Echo probably saw him there each day. Once we explained to Echo that his person had no intention of letting this cat into his home without his approval, and if he felt threatened or wanted to mark his turf, he could use his head and neck to rub his scent around, he resumed using his box.

Physical Resistance/Aggressive Behavior

I have found that most of the time an animal's aggressive behavior stems from pain, both physical and emotional. I have spoken to many people who call me regarding a horse that is bucking, rearing, kicking, pinning ears, etc. The root cause in some of these instances is the fact that the horse is in physical pain of some sort. Once the pain is removed, their temperament changes. Dogs are a bit different, in that they are a very protective species. So if a dog suffered emotional or physical abuse in the past, they may use aggression to make sure it doesn't happen to them again. It is the fear of past pain that drives them. Animals can be overly aggressive towards each other, and there are various reasons for this depending on the animal and situation. Sometimes it is due to jealousy, dominance, insecurity, fear, etc. Finding out the root cause and working towards harmony can help change the undesirable behavior. Giving each animal in the house or barn a job to do gives them an individual purpose to focus on. Dogs that have been attacked by another dog may all of a sudden become aggressive towards other dogs out of fear. If the dog feels that no one is taking the alpha role in the home, they may step up and feel that they need to be dominant, which could result in aggressive behavior when left unchecked or allowed to become out of balance. An animal that is not comfortable in the alpha role may use aggression more often than necessary because they are fearful or insecure. Fear and pain are two main causes of aggressive behavior with domestic animals. When aggression is caused by emotional pain, these animals will require a lot of patience and understanding in order for them to release their emotional trauma and begin to trust again.

Introducing a new Animal

It is always ideal to check to see if the existing animal(s) would like another animal in the home. If you have decided to bring home a new animal, or if you are just fostering an animal for a short time, it helps tremendously to explain to the existing animal(s) that a new animal will be coming into the home and why.

Redefine each of their purposes including how they are

to interact with the new animal (i.e. in addition to your purpose of protecting the house, I have another purpose which is to help maintain harmony in the home and making the new animal feel welcome, teaching them the rules, etc.).

- Confirm the fact that they are not being replaced and that this is a wonderful opportunity for everyone to grow.

- Visualize each of the animals interacting peacefully.

- Rescue Remedy is a good thing to have on hand.

If you do have the opportunity to ask your animals if they would like a companion, take time to figure out what personality type they may want. Do they want a younger or older companion, male or female, dominant or submissive, passive or more playful, etc. Understanding what will make them most comfortable will set you up for a smooth transitional process.

Giving your animals a purpose

When giving an animal a purpose, keep it positive. You don't want to say, "your job is to not chew the rug" (when you say this you picture the animal doing exactly what you don't want them to do). Instead phrase it, "you have an important job in the house and that is to keep everything in order as I left it and if you feel the need to chew on something, please chew your bone, thank you." Acknowledge that the animal did a good job when you return home and this will reinforce the good behavior. You can remind your animal of their job as often as you feel it is needed.

Sending information to an animal is just as important as receiving. Clarity is essential. Keep your thoughts focused and positive. Be true with your word and honor it, this will build trust.

When people call me about a problem they are having with their animal, the first thing I do is take an unbiased view and ask the animal what is going on from their perspective. I give the animals a chance to shed light on what is going on. If I approach a problem telling the animal not to do "it," without really understanding why "it" is happening, then no resolution has been achieved and the animal is still misunderstood. I also find giving the animal a choice gives them an active role in the decision making process which in turn makes them responsible for their behavior. For instance, my cat, Jimmy James Junior, loved being outside. I, however, got nervous when he stayed out after dark and would call and call and he would crouch in the bushes laughing at me and end up staying out half the night. I lost a lot of sleep worrying about him. It finally got to the point where I couldn't do it anymore. I sat down with him and communicated to him exactly what I was feeling, the rules of the house and the choice he had to make. I showed him with my mind's eye the dangers during the night, and how much I worried. I told him that I loved knowing he was safe in the house at night and that he had a choice to make. He could go out all day but had to come in before dark when I called him or if he didn't honor this, I would have to keep him inside until he felt he could keep his end of the bargain. I told him he could go out all day, but I needed him to come running when I called him prior to darkness. I also showed him that when he came in he would get a lot of loving and a special treat.

After that day, without fail, Jimmy James Junior came running when I called him. I used to chuckle because he would come flying out of the woods when I bellowed his name. Sometimes I had to call a few times or give him a chance to get close, but he honored his bargain, and I in turn honored mine.

You can't just tell an animal to do something and expect them to be like a robot and do it. They have to understand why they are doing it and they have to agree to it. We try to initiate compromise and allow the animal to understand our view, as well as understanding and acknowledging theirs.

The Power of positive thinking....

Positive visualization is a major tool in communicating with your animal friend. Whenever we think about something, we give it energy. If we constantly worry about things, we give it energy. When we give something enough energy we create it. That which we fear, we draw near. If thinking about something can actually create it, why not create something we desire or aspire. I have learned this lesson many times the hard way!

Remember, our animals are used to connecting with us telepathically all the time; they are also used to us missing the messages because our minds are too busy or we aren't listening. As a result they resort to other behaviors to get our attention to allow their requests to be heard. Now that you are taking active steps to try to listen to your animals, they may think this is too good to be true, so have patience and remember to be true to your word.

Helping an animal to heal through counseling and flower essences.

As with people, each animal has its own healing calendar. Some heal and move on quicker than others, but that doesn't mean you are helpless. By understanding an animal's past we are helping them to heal. Imagine something terrible happening to you and the people you love most not being able to understand why you are so fearful of certain things and telling you that it is ridiculous. Pretty soon, some animals just shut down or react negatively. Others just keep trying to let us know that certain things bother them.

An animal's past is a blueprint into their present lives, some more so than others, but nonetheless a key to helping your animal move past fear, emotional blocks, and training barriers.

Often times people will contact me to fill in the missing pieces of their animal's past. This is especially true if someone adopted an animal from a shelter or found them as a stray. People want to know what their previous life was like.

Before I owned my horse, Finnegan, he was in training to become a race horse. He had trained at many of the tracks in Massachusetts and upstate New York. Although he had always been a very sensitive horse, he had an accident on the race track that changed the way he looked at things from that day forward. Finnegan had his exercise rider on his back and they were rounding the bend. A large white trash bag flew onto the track and before the rider could steer clear of it, the wind blew it right at Finnegan. He attempted to dodge it at which point the wind pushed it again and it got wrapped around his belly. Horses are prey animals instinctually, so the feeling of some foreign object wrapping itself around his belly was frightening. Finnegan bucked and bucked to get the bag off of him, but instead unseated his rider. She was okay but as she walked over to help him, he got scared again and kicked her in the chest. He became so frightened that his mind was no longer in control and his instincts were in overdrive fighting for his life. Since that day, Finnegan is terrified of anything that moves from the side while he is being ridden. Other horses may have been able to move past this without any lasting effects. Finnegan holds his fears close to him, for fear that if he doesn't he will be caught off guard.

As a result of me knowing this about his past, I can understand where his fears are coming from and try to find different ways of helping him to trust and become less reactive. It has been a long road, but I can honestly say his spookiness has decreased dramatically since I first owned him. Overcoming fear takes time and patience. It does not happen overnight and sometimes major progress is not made for years. Many animals who have been physically abused suffer long term effects that may even manifest themselves into the same aggressive behavior as a means of survival. Knowing what your animal has gone through will help you to understand how to help them and what method of training will be most effective.

Helping an animal with an abusive or traumatic past to heal

Whenever working with an animal that may have had a traumatic past, the first thing you should do is check in on the energy you are projecting. Make sure you shift your energy into a grounded and centered state. This will put a fearful animal more at ease. Then you can acknowledge their pain as something real so that they may now begin to heal.

By understanding their pain, they feel that they don't have to constantly show you that they are afraid of something or fearful of reliving it. Now they feel, you DO understand.

- Acknowledge this and ask your animal what you can do to help them heal.

- Don't put a time frame on healing, allow it to happen at its own pace and don't get discouraged if it takes weeks, months or years. Patience and understanding are essential.

- Don't overwhelm your animal – give them what they need, not what you think they would need.

- Shift your energy to that of a calm leader able to lead the animal away from fear towards a harmonic state of mind.

- See them for who they are and try to focus on their strengths, encouraging them to grow strong and build confidence and a purpose.

- Love, patience, understanding and acceptance are the tools for success.

Things to remember

Traumatic experiences can happen at any stage of an animal's life, and depending on the animal, will affect them differently.

Animals that are taken away from their mother too

young may suffer some anxiety or develop some "strange" habits, i.e., a cat suckling a blanket for comfort, a dog having a hard time understanding other dogs and how to socialize, etc.

Trauma of being attacked by another animal can play out in many ways. Many times I have seen dogs that have been "surprise" attacked by another dog suddenly become aggressive towards other dogs in an attempt to keep themselves from being hurt or taken by surprise again. For some dogs, they become more meek and frightened after such an attack.

Animals like to know their boundaries, especially animals that have been bounced around and had troubled pasts. They need to know the rules and what they need to do. This gives them a purpose, a focus and some stability to their lives. Animals like consistency and a routine. This is especially true of animals that have been abandoned or abused. Many animals that have been abandoned by either their own mother or their people develop a fear of abandonment or separation anxiety. This is why communication, setting a routine, giving your animals reassurance as well as a purpose and a job in your home, will help them resolve these fears.

"My past stalks me and whispers in my ear to be afraid. It is a thorn in my side jabbing me and keeping me ever vigilant."
~ Sam

Bach Flower Essences:

There are many Bach Flower essences that can assist your animal in moving through the healing process for a lot of the situations we discussed above.

The Bach Flower essences are all natural remedies that are made from the essences of various flowers that work in conjunction with our own or the animal's body to balance emotional imbalances. Essences are safe for people and animals. The key is to find the right essence for each situation.

Often times I will get intuitive information as to which essence will help each animal. With practice and your intuition, you will be able to do the same. (There are other companies that have developed Essences for animals besides Bach Flower that also target specific issues.) Below I will discuss a few of the more commonly used essences but I do recommend that the reader educate themselves to all 38 of the Bach Flower essences as well.

How to give flower essences

You can put a few drops in your animal's water bowl, a few drops on a cookie or sugar cube, a few drops directly in their mouth or on their paws. You can also put a few drops on your hands and rub above their eyes, paws, and ears with it.

Many times they will give you a sigh, and then you know it is working.

Flower essences help the animal to heal on an energetic and emotional level. The mistake people make in administering flower essences is that they don't give it often enough or long enough, and they give up on it. You can also combine a few of the flower essences together; however, it is recommended that you do not combine more than six.

Bach Flower Essences:

Rescue Remedy is great before and after a stressful event such as going to the vet, traveling, introducing a new animal, after a traumatic incident, etc. Rescue Remedy is the combination of five of the flower essences:

Star of Bethlehem – for trauma or shock

Clematis – focus, consciousness

Impatiens – nervous, easily agitated, pain and stress

Cherry Plum – to gain control over emotions

Rock Rose – for terror or panic

A few other essences I use often are:

Aspen – for animals that fear a lot of different things, spook easily, hyper alert

Mimulus – for animals that have very specific fears, i.e., fear of loud noises, fear of small spaces, etc.

Vine – for the dominant animal that pushes others around

Beech – for animals that do not tolerate new animals or people in their home and only prefer their owner

Chestnut Bud – to help break bad habits. This remedy also does well when combined with Cherry Plum and Rock Rose during training sessions

Cherry Plum – animals who are high strung, hard to get their attention, can be destructive if their energy doesn't have a focus

Crab Apple – a good remedy for cleansing the body of toxins, painful memories, etc.

Gorse – depression, another good grief remedy

Holly – a good remedy for jealous animals

Impatiens – animals that lack patience

Larch – builds confidence

Olive – animals that are exhausted and lack energy

Pine – a good remedy for grief, missing an animal or

person. Also good for animals that cower or are very submissive, or try too hard to please at their own expense

Vervain – animals with hyper energy that won't relax

Walnut - helps animals feel safe and less vulnerable. Helpful remedy when moving to a new house or barn

Willow – animals that act out when not getting enough attention

Each animal is an individual with a past history and a life purpose that makes them unique. I do not group breeds into certain stereotypes. I view each animal as a unique being. Some animals have vivid memories and hold the abuse from their past very close to them, refusing to let it go for fear that it will only happen again. Other animals live one day at a time and let their past problems float away. They approach life with a fresh uncomplicated view. Some hold fear not necessarily from any present situation, but from a past life experience fearing that they may relive it again.

Some animals are high achievers and eager to please, others don't like to be told what to do and have their own agenda. Some aspire to simply be loved, and others want to be noticed by all. Some animals come here to teach, others to learn and grow. Some animals are old souls and just being in their presence is truly a pleasure.

I have received many calls from frustrated people complaining that their cat is not affectionate, or won't allow them to pick them up and sit quietly on their lap. Animals are individual beings, and like people, some are comfortable with giving and receiving affection and others are not. A very shy person would be completely overwhelmed by someone trying to constantly hug and touch them. The same holds true for animals that feel this way. It does not mean that the animals will remain this way forever but respecting their boundaries will help them to trust quicker. Patience and an understanding of who that animal is and what they are comfortable with, allows them to feel comfortable enough to try to break down the walls they have created for protection. I have found that when people tell their animals they understand they are uncomfortable with being picked up or forced to sit on their lap, etc., and agree not to do this until the animal is ready, allows amazing changes to take place. The animal no longer feels threatened and may even begin to seek out attention and affection.

Counseling Sessions

When dealing with behavioral issues it is always important to hear and understand both sides of the situation and to listen without judgment. Once we find out the cause of the undesirable behavior, we can take steps to help both sides rectify the situation or reach a compromise. Undesirable behavior may be caused by physical problems and/or emotional upset. Sometimes even past life memories can play a part in the health or well being of a present life situation. It is important to be the bridge of information back and forth. I also like to let the animal know that I understand why they are doing what they are doing and I try to let them know why their person is upset with the behavior. I do this through a type of empathy. When we empathize with a person or animal, we are feeling what they are feeling. I take this one step further by sending that feeling to the person or animal I am working with. This way, the animal understands what the person feels when the undesirable behavior is done. After that it is time for resolution or compromise, depending on the situation. I find that you can achieve the desirable behavior a lot faster when both parties agree to compromise with the situation. For instance – I (person) will spend more quiet time with you (cat) if you let me sleep later in the morning. Or... I will greet you first when I come home, if you agree to keep all four feet on the ground when greeting me, etc.

Counseling: **Follow these basic steps to help achieve a positive outcome.**

Bridge – Bridging the gap of understanding between person and animal. Finding out why the undesirable behavior is happening.

Empathetic Relay – Empathize with the animal if there has been any pain, fear, or trauma that is causing the bad behavior. Help them to understand and feel why the bad behavior upsets their person and what the proper behavior is. It is also important to relate to the person's concerns and to help them understand things from the animal's point of view as well. During this stage, especially if the animal has suffered past abuse, has fear issues, etc., I find it necessary to explain to them what a beautiful being they are and that it is important that they feel and accept love and help. I will often times send them a beam of white light and love so that they can feel safe. I speak with them, not as a parent reprimanding a child, but as one loving being to another. I always try to emit a tone of respect, not one of dominance.

Mediator – It is imperative that both sides reach an agreement or compromise so that harmony can be achieved. This is also a good opportunity to find a more acceptable way for the animal to let the person know when they are upset, in pain, frightened, etc.

Reinforce – I like to give the animal a new job in the home that will ultimately reinforce the "Good Behavior" the person desires. This also gives the animal a sense of responsibility and importance.

Replay - I revisit what we talked about during the course of the session highlighting the important facts. I picture the good behavior that is desired and explain what is not acceptable and why. Replay again what their job is and again picture the good behavior. Picture the delight from their person at a job well done. If there was a compromise agreement, I picture that as well and close by honoring and thanking the animal.

Ultimatum - In some severe cases, when a compromise or agreement cannot be reached, we are left with an ultimatum. These are difficult cases, but I find the best way to handle them is to be completely honest with the animal about what the outcome may be with their person if they don't try to change their undesirable behavior. I still complete all the steps listed above, but then I put the ball in the animal's court and allow them to make it their decision based on the information I have given them. I also advise the person what they can do to help their animal make the right choice. For instance, reinforcing and/or rewarding the animal when they are doing their job or are making an effort, etc. It is also important for the person to shift the way they are thinking and how they project their energy and emotion to the animal.

4

HAPPY ANIMALS

There are many ways to use your new animal communication skills to help maintain happy animals. Communication can help alleviate fears and concerns associated with the following scenarios.

Moving

Prior to a move explain to your animals what will be happening and when. Picture for them the new house and yard, so that they can also become excited. Show them that there will be a lot of disruptions during the moving process such as boxes and things being packed up, as well as people who may be coming in and out. If your move involves a long trip it is important to prepare your animals for this.

When I had the daunting task of moving two horses, two goats, one dog, and three cats (two of which had been wild and never confined to a small area before) from Massachusetts to Florida, I put my communication abilities to the test.

My first piece of advice is to tell your animals about the move. In my case, I explained to them what an exciting opportunity this was and that although we all loved our home, we were to embark on a new adventure and a better home. Then tell your animals that you will keep them informed of any new information. Give them time to say goodbye to friends. My horse, Finnegan, becomes very attached to other horses he lives with and it is important for them to know when to say goodbye.

Prior to the move, make sure your animals have updated health records. Some states require this just to enter the state. Make sure each animal has an identification tag, with their name, your name, and emergency contact information. Make sure you have your new address and telephone number on each tag.

As the move approaches, it is important to let your animals know how soon the move will take place, and what is involved. I had to explain to my dog, who hated being in the car that we would be traveling for two and a half days, but we would make frequent stops so that he could stretch his legs and go the bathroom. For the cats, it was even less pleasant. They would have to remain in cat carriers while in the car but would be let out periodically to stretch their legs inside the car, one at a time. I explained to them that we would be staying overnight in hotels and that they would be let out of the cages while in the room, but they must stay away from the door whenever it opened.

Find a pet friendly hotel and it helps to get an interior room, one that doesn't just open into a parking lot. If the room opens into an enclosed hallway, at least your cat can't run far. Take every precaution to ensure the safety of your animals while on the road. Also make sure that the windows inside the room are locked tight. Keep in mind frightened animals can claw and jump through screens.

I used Rescue remedy in spray form and misted the car, cages, animals, myself and the hotel room with it. It worked quite well. Animals may be reluctant to eat or drink while traveling which can bring on other problems. Bring some favorite treats to encourage them to eat. A can of chicken broth is good to have on hand if you are worried that your animal is not drinking water but needs fluid. Bring some bottled water; many times the taste of the water in hotels can put an animal off. Of course always carry your animal's food, a can opener if you feed canned food, and some bowls and plastic utensils.

Moving day is very stressful, and animals can have second thoughts about the whole move, hide or even run away. It is important to secure your animals in a safe area on this day. Many times you will have other people helping and all it takes is a door left open by accident for an animal to escape the chaos and hide.

To make cat carriers more pleasant, I will usually place an object with my scent on it inside the carrier so that the animal smells something familiar, like an old unwashed T-shirt. Try to use a carrier that gives the animal enough room to stand up and stretch out, especially for long trips. Bring the cat carrier out into the open weeks before the trip so that the animal gets used to it.

When you arrive at you final destination, it is important that you allow the animals to get familiar with the house. I recommend that you keep cats in one or two rooms until they understand that this is home and they are not too overwhelmed. I have had many stories of people moving to their new home and not finding their cat for days because they were hiding out somewhere in the home. For dogs, let them see the whole house, and walk them on a leash to inspect the yard and all the new smells. Cats may feel overwhelmed and take a bit longer to adjust than dogs. It is a good idea to keep cats indoors for approximately two weeks so that they have time to feel safe and know that this is their home. When I moved to Florida, I had a whole host of new things to warn my animals about: stay away from the water and the alligators, ignore the frogs (some of the frogs are deadly to dogs), black lizards (poisonous to cats), and stay away from snakes. Explain to your animals the rules and dangers.

When my horses had to make the big move, I had them professionally shipped, and reminded them that we would be waiting at the final destination for them. I also reminded them to drink water any time it was offered. Colic can be a realistic fear with horses that travel long distances and don't drink enough water.

Vacation

Vacations can bring on stress especially if we can't bring

our animals with us. Proper preparation for our animal companions prior to vacation is very important to ensure that we come home to happier animals. This preparation is also extremely helpful in reducing their stress with a new temporary care taker or environment. It is imperative to explain to your animal(s) when and how long you will be gone, where you are going, who will be watching over them, and where they will be staying. Also, it is important to let them know you will be "connecting with them telepathically" while you are away to say hello and check in. Give them a job to do while you are gone, i.e., watch over the house, rest, keep the house in order, watch over the other animals, etc. Picture in your head the day you return and all your animals being so excited and spending some quality time with them. This image will remain with them should they doubt your coming back.

By preparing your animals they will trust you more and know what is going on, instead of feeling deceived and abandoned.

Send your animals mental postcards. This will make them feel like you are still in touch with them and they will enjoy knowing what you are doing. Sounds silly, but they will get your pictures and know you are thinking of them.

Vet Visits

Communication builds trust. Tell the animal about the visit, picture for them what it involves, and a special treat upon returning home or exiting the office. The animal may not be thrilled about going, but at least they won't feel like you tricked them.

Preparing for a show or competition

Animals can read our energy so they know ahead of time what is coming up, but they need to hear it from us to ease some of the anxieties they have. Just because they can sense they are going somewhere doesn't mean they have all the answers. Explain to your animal where you both are going, how long the travel is to get there, and what is expected of them. Picture this for them as vividly as possible. If you are going to be performing an agility course with your dog or a jump course with your horse, use your skills during the event to calm your energy. You can picture the obstacles ahead of time for your animals and give yourself an edge over the competition.

A Change in schedule

Many animals complain that they are feeling insecure and uneasy because their person isn't home as much as they would like. They worry especially if this is not typical and they expect their person home at a certain time. It is important to explain to the animal any change in your schedule so they don't take it personally and worry. Worry is energy that can take the form of negative behavior that essentially could have been avoided with proper communication and compromise. Also, remember if your animal has a lot of stored energy (worry or otherwise), a quick way to release it is through exercise.

One time when I was on vacation I got a frantic call from my pet sitter that my horse, Finnegan, would not come in and eat his dinner. He was standing outside in the sleeting rain and she was worried he may be ill. I connected with him long distance and asked him why he wouldn't come in to the barn to eat. He huffed a bit and then said "I am disgusted; she has been late in feeding us every day." It was true, I usually fed them at 4:00 PM and my pet sitter worked until 6:00 PM. I explained to Finnegan the reason and asked that he please come in to eat and cut the pet sitter some slack until I returned home in four days. Reluctantly, he did make his way back to the barn and ate, but gave the pet sitter the cold shoulder the rest of the week.

New Baby

Explain to your animals the exciting news and let them know how life will change (different noises, smells, schedules, etc.) but that they still have important jobs in your life. Prior to the baby's arrival let the animal explore the baby's room. Prior to bringing baby home, bring the animal something with the baby's scent on it for them to identify. Allow the animal to have an active role in the daily activities with baby. Tell them what you are doing. If you don't allow them to have any part of it, they may not understand and begin to resent your new bundle of joy. Make sure you or your significant other sets aside quiet time with the animals. This helps them to feel important and can be very rewarding for the human as well. I would also explain to the animals the proper behavior with a small child. Never leave a young child or baby alone with an animal. This is for the safety and pleasure of both. I have heard too many stories of dogs and cats that have been sent to a shelter or put down because of a scratch or bite that was essentially provoked by the child unknowingly. We are not talking aggressive animals but if a child lies on top of a dog whose body hurts, or squeezes a cat's neck so that he can't breathe, or pulls a tail, etc., the animal may retaliate physically to get away. This could be avoided if the session was supervised, or the child taught proper behavior around animals.

Picking a Name

Allowing an animal to pick a name is a wonderful way of honoring their essence and intellect. Many times they feel respected right away and will gladly relay to you a name that fits their essence. My good friend, Anne, had a young foal that she asked me to connect with to see what she wanted to be named. I kept hearing Izzy, then Dora, and then it all came through as Izadora. She told me her purpose in this lifetime was to be a graceful dancer. My friend Anne smiled and stated that her goal for this horse was to do Dressage, which is the closest thing to dancing on horseback that you can get! When we arrived at the barn and excitedly told the barn's owner the foal's new name, she asked if we had ever heard the story of Isadora Duncan? We both looked at one another and shook our head. She went on to tell us that it was the true story of a dancer. How did this horse resonate with this name, I will never know. But I don't doubt for a second that all creatures have access to universal knowledge and intelligence that resonates on a soul level.

Izadora

Animals/People Coming or Going

Some animals become quite attached to the friends they make or the people they share their life with. Keep your animal informed whenever you know of an upcoming change that may affect them. Animals can become depressed when their "kids" go off to college, or when dad has to go off to serve in the military, or when Aunt Bea's poodle has to stay for a week. By keeping them informed, they are prepared and trust what the future may bring. My horse, Finnegan, was very attached to a horse he was weaned with. They were best buddies and then one day, this horse was taken out of his paddock and Finnegan never saw him again. He was devastated that he never got to say goodbye. When I purchased him he was very herd bound and became attached to any horse he was put out with. When I moved him home with me, he shared a barn with my neighbor's horse, Peggy, a feisty little Appaloosa mare. She was his girl.

Peggy couldn't be out of his sight for a second or he would become dangerous to himself and others, running frantically, whinnying constantly and working himself into a lather. He threatened to jump the fence many times out of sheer panic. They were best friends for about four years and then one day Peggy's owner told me that they were moving out of state in a few weeks. I relayed this information to Finnegan and, as we got closer to the day she was to leave, I reminded him to say goodbye and wish her well, assuring him that she was embarking on a new journey. On the day the trailer pulled up to take Peggy away, Finnegan watched the whole thing from the paddock. He watched Peggy board the trailer and leave for good. He whinnied once as the trailer door shut but was heartbreakingly silent the rest of the time. He knew she would not return and was prepared because he had a chance to say goodbye which is what so many animals desperately need in order to have closure. I was so proud of him, standing stoic while he was crying inside.

Finnegan

Divorce

Divorce can be disruptive to animals as many times they feel they may have caused the pain or anger they are sensing. They don't know what to do and begin to mirror the energy they see and feel. With proper communication you can alleviate any fears that the animal may have that the cause of the break up is their fault. As long as there is love present, the animal can get through difficult situations easier.

Telepathy Blockers

I have found through my experience that certain things affect the clarity of how I receive information:

- Limit Carbohydrates - (I am a pasta junkie so this was a hard realization!)
- Sweets - You can experience a sugar crash and a decrease in energy.
- "Internal clutter" – Limit internal clutter by quieting the mind, deep breathing, yoga stretches, music, etc., as well as releasing emotional baggage.
- "External clutter" – External clutter can block the delicate free flow of information through our

intuition. Keep your work area as uncluttered as possible. Uncluttering your life has a dramatic effect on you emotionally. A clutter free environment is less overwhelming and emits a feeling of being calm, relaxed and in control.

- Assumptions – Don't assume fish have nothing to say; don't assume a brash cowboy with a bad attitude isn't open to animal communication! People and animals will always surprise you, stay open and try not to assume anything.

    I was introduced to a well known horse trainer who had a bad reputation for being hard on his horses. I immediately assumed he would mock what I do and be too macho to ever use my services. He became one of my best clients, and began to soften his training methods as a result of what his horses communicated!

- Negativity – Don't beat yourself up if you feel you are getting misinformation or feel like you aren't "connecting." We all have off days, allow yourself time to rejuvenate if you feel this way. Do something fun with your animal friends to break out of your negativity.

• Comparing yourself to others – This happens a lot in live workshops. You must remember that each of us is unique and we all have the ability to do this. Some of us may have to work harder than others. Through determination and dedication you will continue to advance and improve. Just continue to believe in this process and in yourself. It is a journey unique to you, so don't compare yourself to anyone else.

• Expecting too much of yourself and the situation can burn you out. You are a translator first and foremost. Do not expect to fix every situation. If you do, you will burn yourself out. Our job is to be a translator so that each side of the partnership understands each other better. Through this understanding, healing can occur and harmony can be achieved.

Enhancing clarity and telepathy

These simple things can enhance your clarity and receptivity.

- Exercise

- Spending time in nature

- Music

- Meditation/Yoga

- Eating a healthy diet – whole foods

- Drinking a lot of water

- Seeking balance – take time for "you" when needed (easier said than done!!)

- Expanding your awareness – take classes to enhance psychic awareness or meditation, etc., read all types of books on the subject, challenging your abilities to go deeper

5

BODY SCANS

The purpose of a body scan is to understand how the animal's body feels and where the weakness or pain may be. Animals are very in tune to their bodies and a body scan is a wonderful way to figure out ways to help them. Just like communication, body scans can be done in person or long distance.

In a body scan we go into the animal's body and experience how their body feels to us. We visualize our energy overlapping into the animal's energy and body. As we pick up subtle pains and feelings in our body, we understand that it corresponds with the animal's body as well. We can also scan the body visually. This is simply viewing the animal's body with your mind's eye and seeing any areas of discomfort, disease or disharmony.

We can also do a body scan by imagining traveling through the animal's body (almost like a laser beam) and actually looking inside each area. What we are looking for when we do this "viewing" is any area that pulls our attention to it, and may look irregular. What is irregular? It can be a color that doesn't feel right, an energy block or another symbol or feeling that signals something is wrong. You may also hear certain words as you scan the body, such as hot, working hard, imbalance, pain in chest, stomach ache, etc. You may also begin to feel things in your body, pay attention to everything you get.

The other technique I use to find out where an animal hurts is to ask them to picture themselves moving so I can "see" what areas are of concern. Many times an animal will be very dramatic in showing you where they hurt by zooming in on a leg or body part in your mind's eye or holding up a leg to show you it hurts. Sometimes you will just hear, my foot hurts, etc. I ask animals to show me themselves moving in my mind's eye so that I can observe where the problem may be. Horses that jump will show me at what point they feel pain while jumping. They may also zoom in on a particular body part to let me know that it is the source of pain. It is like a movie playing in my head, and I am simply observing the film. The animal is the director and the star and I am taking notes.

Observe it all. Take your time and explore. The more you do it and receive feedback, the more you will understand how you are getting the information. Feedback and validation is vital to your continued growth.

Things to remember:

- Take note of any pain you may feel in your physical body prior to starting so that you don't mistake that for the animal. If an animal has pain in the same area as you, often times the pain will become noticeably more intense. It takes practice to turn these subtle sensations into stronger interpretations.

- Asking permission – Make sure you ask the animal if you can scan their body for pain. I explain to them that their people want to help them feel better and I ask the animal to send me any areas that hurt. If you prefer not to "feel" this, you can ask them to zoom in on the areas of their body that hurt or are a concern. so that you see instead of feel it.

- See it, feel it, sense it - You can get health information in a variety of ways, make sure you write down whatever you get in any form you get it, so that it can be validated.

- Colors – Colors can have a specific meaning. Take note if you see an organ in a certain color, or if parts of the body glow red, etc. Here are some examples of what colors can mean: (red– heat; black – toxic or problematic; green - needs healing). What do the colors mean to you? With practice and validation you will develop your own vocabulary to draw upon.

- Feelings – Pay attention to the slightest sensation in your body; a tingle, a brushing feeling, a twitch, fast heartbeat, labored breathing, ears hurting, eyes blurred, skin itchy, stomach aches, instant headache, tingle in elbow, etc.

- Seeing – See the animal moving; see where they are lame or off. They may even zoom in on a body part for you.

- Hearing – They may say a word such as "eyes." Or you may hear "I am concerned about my eyes," "I have trouble going to the bathroom," etc.

- Make your way through the body and if you don't get anything initially, start at the head and work your way back.

- Write down anything you get.

- **Remember to describe what you get – don't diagnose. We are not Veterinarians; we are simply trying to understand from the animal's point of view what is wrong. This information can be used to assist your vet if needed.**

- If you have lingering pain, or feel lightheaded, ground yourself by walking around, touching the earth, eating, in addition to surrounding yourself in white light. Imagine roots growing out of your feet into the earth and breathe in the energy of the earth through the body and out the top of your head.

Body Scan Examples

- Mystery illness – I had a client call me about her young horse. All four of the horse's legs were swollen and the vet could not figure out why. When I connected with the horse and asked him about this, he showed me that he had a white supplement that was added to his feed. I immediately felt that he was allergic to it. When I told the person this, she said that recently he was put on a daily wormer that is added to his feed, and it is white. When she removed this from his feed, his swelling disappeared!

- Emotional pain – A client called me about her beautiful gray bird that was pulling out his feathers. He was a newcomer to the family and she feared that he was not happy. When asked why, he exclaimed that he was hoping that if he pulled out his feathers they would grow back green. The other birds in the home were green and he wanted to be like them. The person confirmed that she had two green parrots in the home that had been with her for a very long time. With a little counseling and an effort on the person's part to tell Ollie how beautiful his "gray" feathers were, his feather pulling days became fewer and fewer.

Disease serves many purposes that you may not know. It challenges the very spirit to a war of wills, faith and tolerance. It is one of our greatest lessons here on earth.

It helps to understand the anatomy of an animal if you want to enhance your abilities and become more specific in your interpretations. You can pull up many animal anatomy charts online.

Body Scan Exercises:

The best way to learn is to just get in there and do it.

You can use the body scan worksheet as a guide or you can simply develop your own style of going through the body.

Body Scan – worksheet

Head:

Eyes:

Ears:

Nose:

Mouth:

Teeth:

Glands:

Throat:

Neck:

Shoulders:

Legs: (front, back, and joints)

Paws/hooves:

Back:

Rump:

Tail:

Lungs/Breathing:

Heart/Stamina:

Stomach:

Intestines:

Liver:

Kidneys:

Spleen:

Pancreas:

Blood:

Other Organs:

Spirit/Outlook:

Emotions:

Additional Questions to ask

What things help?

What things affect health negatively?

Is there an energy block that needs to be cleared?

What can be done to rebalance the body?

How is the food?

Water?

Supplements?

We are a species made up of heart and pride. We work through our pain so that we can continue to please. We may not be as good as we once were but we try hard to do what we once did. We don't wish to disappoint. We work through the pain and suffer silently later.

6

DEEPENING THE CONNECTION

Certain things must be present within yourself to access telepathy successfully such as love, trust, and honor for yourself and others.

We receive information from the animals in a variety of different ways. It is like a ball of energy that we "translate and interpret." Distinguishing between your own mental clutter and that of the animal is the ongoing challenge of telepathic communication.

It is important to put your own fears, beliefs and baggage aside. When another being is speaking we must practice being present and listening. This is more difficult than it sounds. During a telepathic connection, being present is a very important building block to success.

Telepathic communication is a partnership. It is important for the communicator to trust what the animal wishes to be known even if it is not what the question was. Do not be too hard on yourself and feel gratitude for the opportunity to communicate with these beings. Continue to grow and expand by using your telepathic muscle daily.

Exercise:

Questions for your animal teacher – deepening the connection

You will need an animal teacher to work with. Try to use

an animal you may not know too much about.

Animal's Name:

<u>QUESTIONS:</u>

What is your personality like? Show me/tell me.

What is your advice for me?

Can you tell me about your purpose?

Can you tell me about your past?

What do you like/dislike about your environment?

Do you have any physical ailments/pain? Tell me about it? Where does it hurt, how does it feel, how did it happen?

What can be done to help you?

What lessons do you still have to learn or teach?

What do you like most about being a (type of animal)?

What is your fondest memory?

What do you have to teach me today?

What can you tell me about your past lives?

Is there anything you'd rather be doing or wish to do?

Do you have any complaints?

What lessons have you learned about life as a (type of animal)?

How can I improve my telepathic ability with animals?

Do you have a message for me?

Thank your animal teacher.

Animals have a lot to teach us.

I encourage you to begin communicating with the animals in your life and those who cross your path. They may have something quite amazing to share with you.

Visit a local animal sanctuary, or just sit in nature and see who pops up. Connect with the animals and have a pen and paper handy to allow their thoughts to flow through you.

Exercise:

Heart to heart and soul to soul.

Animal's name:

Take a minute to write down why you felt this animal has such an impact on your life and your heart.

What purpose do you feel this animal had in this lifetime and in your life?

What do you think the animal may have learned from being in your life?

Take a moment to comment on this animal's;

Physical essence:

Spiritual essence:

Emotional Essence:

If the animal is still in his/her physical body, be sure to take some time to relay the information you wrote down to your animal friend. Just sit and talk to him/her about it.

If your animal is in spirit, take a moment when you won't be disturbed to honor his/her life with you. Light a candle, sit quietly, and intend to connect with the energy of your animal friend in spirit – then explain to them the impact they had on your life. Take a moment to feel their love around you then thank them and send them love.

Animals come into our lives for many reasons. It is important to understand the depth of soul each animal possesses. This is an important step in understanding the spiritual essence that animals have. Animals have an unselfish love and many times will put themselves in a difficult situation to help their people learn something they need in this lifetime.

Exercise:

You will need to use a friend's or relative's animal for this exercise. Pick an animal teacher that you don't know much about their living space and make sure their person is willing to validate the details for you. Connect as outlined earlier and ask the animal to show you their home or ask permission to enter their body and look through their eyes. This practice will give you confidence when working with lost animals. Ask them to show you where they eat, sleep, if they have a fenced yard, if the house is one or two stories, what the floors are made of, where their favorite spot to nap is, etc. Have fun with this.

Exercise:

Go to a local animal preserve. Connect with a few of the animals there. Allow their awareness and spiritual essence to come through. Ask them about their life story, their struggles, their likes and dislikes.

Developing Other Psychic Skills

Exercise:

Play the psychic for a day game

For one full day, tune in and listen to your intuition with everything you do from picking out what to eat, deciding what route to take, what the weather will be like, who is on the phone, which team will win tomorrow, or what book to read next, etc. Have fun with this and really try to trust your intuition. Any questions that arise during the day, allow your intuition to decide. Do this one day each week. Remember to log in your progress.

Exercise:

Sending messages/the telephone game

This is a fun experiment to try when you have a free moment. Pick someone who calls often enough but not someone who phones you daily. Sit quietly, close your eyes and focus on the friend you choose. Say his/her name in your head and picture them in your mind's eye. Tell them to call you telepathically. Envision him/her thinking of you, and slowly envision him/her looking at the phone and taking steps to call you. Picture every detail of the scene right down to punching in your number on the phone. Imagine hearing yourself answer the phone saying "hi," etc. When you are done, write down the time you ended the exercise. Then don't think about it anymore. See what happens. If your friend calls, ask her what she was doing at the time of the exercise. If she doesn't call, call her the next day and ask her how her day was yesterday and if she thought of calling you. Sometimes they get the message but don't have a free minute to call. Try this exercise a few times, once with the same person and another time with someone else.

Two of the most common questions I get from my students are:

1. How do I tell if it is my logical mind or my intuition?

2. How do I tell if I am making it up?

I will answer the second question first. Trust what you get. Most times intuition comes through our imagination. So, if your logical mind is questioning it, chances are you are using your intuition. Try this exercise: Say your name a few times in your head. Pay attention to how it feels. Does it feel right, true, real? Now say someone else's name, my name is (someone else's name), and see how this feels. Your body knows truth. If it is false, it will not flow easily and may feel uncomfortable. Pay attention to this subtle way of knowing truth. Okay, in answer to the first question....the logical and intuitive mind think very differently. The logical mind comes from an ego point of reference, and the intuitive mind comes from a higher/soul wisdom. Here is a breakdown of the differences:

Logical Mind	Intuitive Mind
Slow	Fast
Judges	Accepts
Critical	Loving
Controlling	Flowing

Needs proof	Trusts
Limiting	Full of Potential
Complex	Simple
Thinking	Flowing
Driven	Calm
Doubts	Allows
Guilt	Forgives
Attached to outcome	Detached
Protective	Adventurous

Code of Ethics

There is a code of ethics that a lot of communicators work with. Please take a minute to read the code of ethics listed below:

CODE OF ETHICS for INTERSPECIES TELEPATHIC COMMUNICATORS

Formulated in 1990 by Penelope Smith

Our motivation is compassion for all beings and a desire to help all species understand each other better, particularly to help restore the lost human ability to freely and directly communicate with other species.

We honor those that come to us for help, not judging, condemning, or invalidating them for their mistakes or misunderstanding but honoring their desire for change and harmony.

We know that to keep this work as pure and harmonious as possible requires that we continually grow spiritually. We realize that telepathic communication can be clouded or overlaid by our own unfulfilled emotions, critical judgments, or lack of love for self and others. We walk in humility, willing to recognize and clear up our own errors in understanding others' communication (human and non-human alike).

We cultivate knowledge and understanding of the

151

dynamics of human, non-human, and interspecies behavior and relationships, to increase the good results of our work. We get whatever education and/or personal help we need to do our work effectively, with compassion, respect, joy, and harmony.

We seek to draw out the best in everyone and increase understanding toward mutual resolution of problems. We go only where we are asked to help, so that others are receptive and we truly can help. We respect the feelings and ideas of others and work for interspecies understanding, not pitting one side against another but walking with compassion for all. We acknowledge the things that we cannot change and continue where our work can be most effective.

We respect the privacy of people and animal companions we work with, and honor their desire for confidentiality.

While doing our best to help, we allow others their own dignity and help them to help their animal companions. We cultivate understanding and ability in others, rather than dependence on our ability. We offer people ways to be involved in understanding and growth with their fellow beings of other species.

We acknowledge our limitations, seeking help from other professionals as needed. It is not our job to name and treat diseases, and we refer people to veterinarians for diagnosis of physical illness. We may relay animals' ideas, feelings, pains, symptoms, as they describe them or as we feel or perceive them and this may be helpful to veterinary health professionals. We may also assist through handling of stresses, counseling, and other gentle healing methods. We let clients decide for themselves how to work with healing their animal companions' distress, disease, or injury, given all the information available.

The goal of any consultation, lecture, workshop, or interspecies experience is more communication, balance, compassion, understanding, and communion among all beings. We follow our heart, honoring the spirit and life of all beings as one.

7

ANIMALS IN SPIRIT

Grieving for an animal can be one of the most difficult things to get through. Many people who do not have animals do not understand. Seek support from others who understand. Grief is a process. Allow yourself time to grieve and in time make a commitment to move forward and heal. This doesn't mean you are forgetting about your animal, it means that you are honoring what they would want.

Many people can't let go of their animal's physical presence and hold on to their grief not wanting to heal. Animals report that this inhibits them from growing on the other side when their person is unable to let go. It keeps them more earthbound fearing they are needed. Remember to acknowledge the grief the other animals in the home may be going through as well. Try to grieve and heal together, understanding each animal's unique way of handling it. Know that love transcends all boundaries and you will be reunited again! It is the ones left behind who have the hardest part ahead of them, your animal friend in spirit is in good hands and pain free.

Death is a decision made on the soul level. There is a purpose and divine pattern to why and when an animal's soul has decided to pass. We question it, and sometimes are consumed with guilt: Did I do enough? Were they ready? Did I wait too long? Were they in pain? This process can be a season of growth for us as well as the animal. Trust in this process as difficult as it may be and allow your heart to heal; it is truly what the animal wants. Staying in a place of guilt and grief will hold you and your animal back from the process of divine growth. When the soul is set free from the restrictions of a body, it is a rebirth of freedom and bliss. They are still with us, and we will be together again.

Death is a transition. The spirit and personality continue on, it is just the physical body that is shed. Once an animal or person transitions into spirit, it doesn't mean they are gone. We may not be able to reach out and touch or see them but know they are there and ready to help us if we need them. Animals tell me all the time how much fun it is in spirit form because now they can go with their people everywhere.

I had the pleasure of doing a consultation with a little white pony named Nikki. Nikki had passed into spirit after a traumatic experience. Nikki's people, Donna and Rainey, wanted me to connect with her to see how she was doing on the other side. Donna was worried that her daughter was having a hard time with Nikki's death.

When I connected with Nikki the pony, she told me that she was doing fine but that she was worried about

Rainey. Nikki the pony said that she visits Rainey every night and showed me that she went into Rainey's room. (Nikki showed me that Rainey's room had carousel horses all around, and that Rainey kept a tuft of Nikki's tail hair hung in her closet and that she would often go over and touch the tail hair and cry). When I relayed this information to both Donna and Rainey, Rainey perked up. She said that her room did have carousel horses and that she did keep a tuft of Nikki's tail hung up in her closet. Rainey thought it so cool that her pony was in her bedroom. Rainey eagerly asked if Nikki had accompanied her to her trip to New York. When I went back and asked Nikki, she said of course. I asked Nikki how Rainey would know she was there and Nikki showed me that Rainey had peppermints in the pockets of her jacket. Rainey burst out laughing and said that it was indeed true, they were Nikki's favorite treats.

It was comforting for Rainey and Donna to know that even though their beloved pony, Nikki, had passed into spirit, she was still with them and enjoying their company in spirit form.

Animals can also show you who they are with on the other side:

Example:

I got a call from a woman name Victoria. Victoria had contacted me about her dog, CC, who passed into spirit a few months prior. When I connected with CC, he was excited to share information about his new world. Victoria wanted to know who he was with on the other side. When I asked CC this he began to show me a picture of a woman who was missing a hand, a small man with a flannel shirt on, and toy trains all around him. When I relayed this information to Victoria, she was silent. I began to sweat a bit, silence isn't always a good thing! Then she broke the silence and said that CC was with her parents. Her dad was a small man that collected toy trains, and her mom had come to her in a dream after she had passed and in the dream she only had one hand. For Victoria, this was a double confirmation that her dog was being well taken care of with her parents on the other side, and validation that her mother had communicated with her from spirit through a dream. There is great comfort in knowing that our animals have friends and relatives on the other side waiting for them. Trust that your animals are in good hands on the other side.

Many people want validation that their animal in spirit is still around them. Sometimes the signs are quite obvious, other times we have to trust. Animals will often visit us in dreams after they have passed. It is the easiest way for them to communicate with us from spirit. Many times they visit just to let us know they are okay. Many animals that I have communicated with in spirit show me things a person is going through presently, a new hair cut, or an upcoming trip they are going on, etc. This is their way of letting you know they are still a part of your life. When they just pop into your mind out of the blue, take a moment to say hello to them because chances are their spirit is with you. Have fun with them and know that they are never far.

How to know when your animal is ready to pass over:

This is a very difficult subject and the source of many calls. How do we honor our animals and know when they are ready to pass over? How do we know if they want help passing over or if they want to pass on their own? Each animal has a unique plan and honoring this process can be difficult especially when our emotions and fears are running high. Here are a few things to consider during this process:

Animals view death much differently than we do. They somehow are able to see the big picture and understand or maybe remember where it is they came from in the spirit realm. They understand that death may be a process and part of an experience that all will learn from.

It is true that the eyes are the window to the soul, and

many times you can tell just by looking into your animal's eyes if the spirit is fully present in the body or preparing to leave. There is a vacancy to an animal's eye when they are prepared to pass into spirit. Give your animal permission to leave and let them know you will be okay. I have worked with so many animals that hold on in a sick body because they are so worried about their people or they are not sure who is going to fill their role. By talking to your animal about this and relieving them of this fear the spirit becomes less tethered to the physical realm and can transition easier. It is important that you say this and also mean it from your heart. Allow your animal to make the journey with all the love in your heart. Death is a transition out of the physical body, it is freeing the spirit. It is not something to be feared.

When I connect with an animal that is close to passing, I will often see angels all around them. You can pray to the angels to help your animal and let you know when it is time to step in and help. If you have time with your animal prior to them passing into spirit, they love to hear about the good times you had together and what they taught you. This helps them to feel fulfilled in their purpose here and in your life. Don't dwell on the sick body; this creates a heavy energy that the spirit finds hard to move through. Remember to prepare the other animals in the home and keep them informed. I have seen many animals, as they are preparing to pass into spirit, have a one on one conversation with one of the animals in the home or barn. It is my understanding that they are assigning or discussing who will be next in charge or to fill their role. My dog, Champ, had a meeting of the minds prior to his passing. He and my cat, Ernie, sat together as Champ assigned Ernie the role of boss of the home after he passed. Ernie, to this day, does not let anyone forget that. He rules with an iron paw.

"Don't mess with the king"
~ ERNESTO VITO

Should you have to help your animal pass over, try to be with them during this process. Some animals will also request to pass at home and some vets now make house calls for this very reason. If your only alternative is to go into the vet's office, you can make your animal more comfortable by bringing a familiar blanket or bed for them to lie on during the process. Use Rescue Remedy for both you and your animal. Touch your animal throughout the process knowing that it is a transition and that they are never really gone. Some animals will pass on their own and will do it specifically when you are not around. Animals tell me it is easier for them to pass when it is quiet and emotions are not running high. People tend to hold a lot of guilt when an animal passes and they are not there, but know that many times this is a conscious choice.

Reincarnation

A frequent question people ask me to ask their animals in spirit is whether or not the animal will incarnate back into their lives, and if so as what. Some animals choose to rejoin their person's life as another animal. Many people report that the new animal has similar personality traits as the animal that had passed. Some animals prefer to work with their people from spirit and wait for them to join them when their time comes. Other animals may choose to come back as a wild animal to learn a new lesson in a new body.

How will I find my animal if they have

reincarnated?

Sometimes the animal is very specific as to what they are coming back as and how it will happen, right down to specific markings to help you identify them.

My friend and co-author of Untamed Voices, Sue Steffens, had a Tiger who told us after he had passed that he would be coming back as a white Tiger cub and that Sue would know that it was him because he would have unusually BIG feet. What an odd thing to say we thought. Sure enough, Sue was given the opportunity to adopt a gorgeous white Tiger Cub, and the first thing that everyone said when they met him was, "WOW, what big feet."

Where do animals go when they pass?

Animals can share with us what they are doing on the other side and what it looks like. They will also let us know who they are with. Sometimes they are running free in places similar to what they enjoyed here on earth, without pain or fear. Some animals are proud to share with us the job they are doing on the other side, and others balance their time between the two dimensions so they can continue to spend time with their people.

How to communicate with an animal in spirit:

- Breathe three cleansing breaths and connect with God's love by saying a prayer or opening your heart to universal love. Feel this love fill your body. Then you can begin as usual....

- Go through the steps as outlined before - The communication may be more difficult in the beginning especially if you are communicating with an animal whose person is still very emotional or upset. High emotions can hinder the flow of information at times. This is also why lost animal cases can be so difficult.

- Offer gratitude for this experience.

- Make sure you ground yourself and protect your energy afterwards.

Communication Exercises with Animals in Spirit

Exercise:

You can use the following questions to connect with the animal if you wish, or just see what they have to say.

Questions for your animal teacher in spirit:

Tell me about where you are.

Who are you with?

How did you pass?

Will you come back, if so as what?

Do you have a message?

Do you have a job over there, if so can you tell me about it?

Did you have a job or purpose while you were on the earth plane?

Thank you.

Exercise:

Pick a morning or evening when you won't be interrupted to set aside 15 minutes to do the next exercise.

- Pick an area you feel most comfortable – inside or outside.

- Take three cleansing breaths.

- You can put on music if you like or enjoy the

silence.

- Set your intention to have one or more of your animals in spirit to come forward.

- When one of your animals pops into your head – imagine them with your mind's eye sitting in front of you.

- Imagine yourself reaching forward and patting them.

- Imagine you smell, feel, see and hear them.

- Take a minute to express whatever it is that you want to say to them.

- Then ask them if they have a message for you.

- You can continue to ask them questions if you like or you can just enjoy being with them.

- When done, thank them for helping you to connect with them in this way.

I find it comforting to think that when an animal passes they cross a rainbow bridge to the other side that is so full of vibrant colors, beautiful sounds and loving friends that it is pure joy. We can cross this bridge any time in our mind or through our dreams to visit our animal friends. And when our time comes, they will be there to greet us upon our arrival.

Here is a paragraph from the book "Untamed Voices" about the process of passing into spirit from an animal's perspective:

Can you tell me what it is like being in spirit?

"What I distinctly remember about shifting out of my body is the feeling of being weightless.   I felt as if I was in a hollow tunnel, and it seemed to echo.   I began thinking about when I was a young cub.   I was quite small and I could see my mother.   Then I felt immediately filled with what I can describe as a type of exhilaration and excitement.   At that moment everything sparkled and glowed.   I felt like a cub as I awoke to a realm of beauty.   My mother was there, she licked me.   I was at home, and I felt at peace.   I did not sit still for long, and I began to explore. There were limitless things to see. If I thought I would like to walk by the mountain, I was instantly in that place. My lungs were full of the breath of light, and I have never felt better. I relived everything I had ever done."

8

LOST ANIMALS

Connecting with a lost animal, can be challenging at best. Because there is so much emotion, fear, and panic on the part of the person as well as the animal, the connection can be hard to receive. Information may come in bits and pieces, it may not necessarily come in chronological order and the animal may not realize if they are still alive or have passed over into spirit. Despite these bumps, there are many success stories of telepathic communication bringing lost pets and their humans back together. By learning how to connect to a lost animal, you will be able to help friends and neighbors in the event that their animal is missing.

Lost animal cases are very difficult for many reasons:

- There is a lot of emotion and fear involved which can hamper the accuracy and clarity of the signal.

- Time is of the essence, there can be panic and static which can be a result of this.

- We put a lot of pressure on ourselves to "get it right." This sabotages the intuitive nature of the communication.

- Personal boundaries can be overlooked when working on these cases.

- Information may not come in chronological order creating a lot of frustration for the person, animal and you.

- Having said this, lost animal cases can also be quite rewarding when an animal and their person are reunited.

Important questions to ask:

☐ Are you in your body?

☐ Can you hear anything?

☐ What does the ground feel like under your feet?

☐ Can you see light?

☐ Can I look through your eyes, look around for me?

☐ How did you get here, can you show me how?

☐ When you left your house which direction did you go?

☐ Print out a map of the area – try to feel the energy of the animal on the map.

☐ Don't be afraid to try using other methods of connecting, e.g., use a picture if you think it may help.

☐ How does your body feel?

☐ Did you leave for a reason?

☐ Do you want to come home?

☐ Do you have a message for your person?

How do you tell if an animal is alive or in spirit?

☐ If the animal passed out of his/her body suddenly, they may not be aware that they have left their body. In situations like this, we can help the animal to make the transition with love and compassion and tell them to go to the light.

☐ You may get physical impressions when you connect with the animal indicating that they are in their body – the feeling of them being hungry or thirsty, seeing them running, etc. This is a good indication that they are in their body.

☐ You may get a feeling of peacefulness which could indicate they are in spirit.

☐ You may see the animal looking down at their

body as if they are hovering above; this is a good indication that their soul has left the body.

☐ You may see angels with the animal, another indication the animal may be in spirit.

☐ When I first started doing this work, I had one case where I connected with the animal and saw them looking down upon their body on the side of the road, I was not sure if the animal was dead or not and then asked for more information, I then got the strong taste of blood in my mouth.

Different techniques used to locate lost animals:

☐ Go into their body and ask to see through their eyes to sense what they sense. This will allow you to see what is around them. It may give you valuable clues as to where they are.

☐ Remote viewing is the practice of receiving information about a subject or target using ESP (Extra Sensory Perception), which is using your intuition on a broader scale to see where the animal is. It is as if you are there looking at the animal and the surrounding area.

☐ Dowsing is the ability to sense the energy of an animal, person, object, etc., using a dowsing tool. You can fine tune this ability so that you can actually sense the energy of a missing animal using a map. You can use your finger or another device as a tool. Pendulums are often the tool of choice.

☐ Ask other animals in the home if they know where the animal is.

☐ Ask for help from your spirit guides and power animals.

☐ Ask for information to come in dreams.

It is important to give the person something to do in addition to looking for their animal.

Empower them with these ideas:

1.) Imagine a golden cord going from your heart to that of the animal you are trying to locate. Send love and courage through this cord of energy to channel to your animal. Do not overwhelm the animal with worry, simply send love. (Many times animals will use this "energy channel" to find their way home, use the energy to help heal themselves if they are tired or scared, and in the case of cats who are not lost but may be out on an extended hunting trip, encourage them to return sooner).

2.) Lost dogs can travel incredibly far. Contact shelters and pounds in the surrounding towns. Don't just limit it to your town.

3.) Make flyers with your animal's picture and talk to all

your neighbors. Many lost animals are located this way.

4.) It has been my experience that dogs can actually get lost and lose track of where they are. Cats are very good at finding their way home; it is usually something that scares them that keeps them away, such as another cat or wild animal or dog that chased them out of their area. Some animals leave home for other reasons and are not actually "lost." These reasons differ with each animal. Some common reasons that animals have told me they have left are: "The house has been too busy lately and I need some quiet time!" This is a common scenario with cats around the holiday season or if guests "invade" their home. Many animals are social beings and will wander to visit other animals in the surrounding area. A great tip to help find a dog that has run off, especially in an area away from home, is to place a crate with an old shirt or article of clothing with your scent on it in the area the animal went missing. Place a bowl with water in there as well. (Don't put food in there as it may attract other animals). Come back to the spot often to see if the dog has returned. Sometimes animals will leave a stressful situation seeking out a new home. I have also had animals tell me that they will only return if their person takes better care of their self, i.e., stops smoking, etc. Nothing surprises me anymore!

5.) I also advise people to ask for information about their animals to come to them as dreams. Animals communicate with us all the time, but if our minds are too busy we may not get their messages. When we dream, information streams in uninterrupted. Before you go to bed at night write down a question you want an answer to: For example - I wish to get information on where my kitty is and if she is okay. Then state this intention before you go to sleep and ask to remember your dreams (very important). Your animal may just waltz into one of your dreams looking vibrant and healthy letting you know they are okay, or they may appear in an area that your forgot to look letting you know that they are stuck, etc. Dreams can be quite profound and informative.

Examples of some lost animal cases:

Ober was a big sweet tuxedo cat who was strictly an indoor kitty. His owner, Sue, called me upset that Ober had gotten out the door and had not returned and now it was over a week that he was missing. When I connected with Ober, his sweet teddy bear energy came through. I explained to him that I had his person on the line and she was searching desperately for him. He showed me that he was under something low, like a crawl space or porch and there was sand or dirt under his feet. He proceeded to send me pictures of how he scooted through a narrow opening to get under there after being chased by another cat. He was quite scared and didn't know how to get back out. He showed me which direction he ran from the house which helped Sue know what direction to look in. The next day Sue let me know that she found him hiding under a porch and was able to coax him out just with her voice. I love happy endings!

Mirabella – Tortoise Shell Cat

I adopted a blind kitty named Mirabella a few years ago and she has become quite the "Spit Fire." I had to have an intervention with her because she kept running out the door every chance she got and I feared for her safety. She defiantly told me this:

"My lack of sight will not stop me from being all cat and that is why I run outside every chance I get. I still want to experience all the pleasure that being outside has to offer. It is like a party for my senses."

Do you realize how dangerous being outside is for a blind cat, and that you must stay inside and appreciate it safely from behind a screen?

"Just try to stop me. I don't accept 'no'."

Three days after this conversation with Mirabella, she somehow slipped out of the house late one evening when we were letting the dogs in. I never realized she was missing until the morning when she did not come greet me with her morning chatter. My heart sank as I frantically searched the house for her. I quickly realized she was not stuck somewhere in the home, but must have escaped out the door. That means this vulnerable blind kitty was out all night. My husband and I searched for two days, walking the neighborhood and woods. I was slowly losing faith and fearing the worst. Friends all felt she was alive and close, but I was too filled with fear to trust my connection and know for sure. Then I heard a voice say "Do you believe in miracles?" It was not Mirabella's voice but a voice from my guides I believe. I kept hearing it through the day. That night my husband and I concentrated on searching the woods and

to my delight I saw her beautiful face emerge. She was stuck in the woods underneath all the underbrush and brambles, and every time she tried to move, she felt trapped by the overgrown earth. Her voice was just too parched to call out to me when I called to her. That night I thanked God for small miracles. You may think that after such a scare Mirabella would steer clear of the doors, quite the contrary!

9

COMMUNICATING WITH WILD ANIMALS

I have found that connecting with wild animals can be slightly different than connecting with domesticated animals as they are more instinctual by nature and can be less willing to "talk" just for the sake of talking. Their communication can be a bit slower in coming through especially if they feel threatened. Their sense of survival is very well preserved and their trust level is reserved thus making it a bit more difficult sometimes in getting the communication started and flowing effectively. They are masters at reading the energy we project. I have, however, seen quite the opposite, depending on the species. Dolphins are a good example of a wild mammal that loves to communicate. Every Dolphin that I have communicated with has been extraordinary in their ability and desire to communicate with us.

Suggestions when working with wild animals:

- It is imperative that you diffuse your energy so that your presence is not overwhelming to the animal. Do this by grounding yourself and softening your energy – imagine a soft pink light around your body like a fine mist, not a bright light. Take a few deep breaths, allow any tension or anxiety to flow out of your fingertips and toes.

- Imagine yourself as that animal and in doing so you may get specific sensations or emotions that the animal is feeling.

- One of the best ways to practice connecting with wild animals is to go on a Field Trip! Remember as a kid what fun you had going on a day adventure!!!! Well, pack up a lunch, a notebook, and bring along your inner child – it is time for a Field Trip! Plan a trip to:

☐ Animal Sanctuary or Shelter

☐ Wildlife Rehab or Rescue

☐ Nature Park

☐ Bird Sanctuary

☐ Aquarium

☐ Zoo

Depending on the place you choose, you may encounter some animals that are unhappy, so be prepared for this. Some animals are perfectly content and thankful to be in a place where they know they are being taken care of. Don't prejudge the situation; go in with an open mind. I like to honor each animal I encounter in such a place. See each animal with dignity and send them a lot of love. Be sure to ground yourself when you leave and protect your energy. You may be haunted by some of the emotion you may feel there, but in return you can offer something that many other people can't who go to see the animals there. You can lend them an ear, and really listen and care.

In the book, *Untamed Voices*, I had the pleasure of touring many wonderful animal sanctuaries and preserves. My coauthor, Sue Steffens, owns a remarkable preserve called *Tigers For Tomorrow* in Alabama. I have had the honor of working with some of the world's most exotic animals there who were happy to talk and share some of their deepest thoughts, desires, and fears. Here are some stories from that book:

Benny – Black Leopard

"I want people to know that we are all different. Please do not link us all into the same category just because we are of one species. Just like humans, we have different experiences and souls. Most people just look and observe. Only a few ever really "talk" to us and ask us what we are about, why we are here. This is where we will start. My story is simple – it is about me, a girl, and

189

a vision that merged into one. We saw a world created to dignify the throwaways. How can some of the mightiest and rarest beasts on earth be treated with such malice and disrespect? This is where our story starts.

"When the animals come here, they are suddenly dignified and important. They are no longer throwaways; they become the cell, the organs and the oxygen in a world where we are the focus. It is truly a world of our own, where we are the masters.

"When we eat the flesh of another being it is just that. We are not eating your soul or your essence or your personality, no it is just flesh. In a hunt, the predator can sometimes see the soul of our prey leave the body before the body dies. In a way, we are allowing the soul to fly.

"In order to create a new tomorrow, people need to feel their souls again and experience the heartbeat of life. They need to know the ties that unite us all. Do people understand that treating just one being with disrespect and hate creates a blemish and a hole in the soul of existence? That cannot be undone. Love is the true source of life and joy."

Lakota – Gray Wolf in Spirit

Lakota is a very wise being. I had the pleasure of knowing her when she was in her physical body. Towards the end of her physical life here, Lakota had a specific message for Sue. She wanted her to know that although her body was very ill, she could not leave until Sue understood that she would be getting three juvenile wolves who would be the divine ones and they were meant to take over her wolf enclosure after she leaves this earth. She also explained that when she was ready to pass into spirit Sue would know because the earth would shake. Once the three wolves had been found, Lakota began to let go of her earthly ties. Sue stayed by Lakota's side during this time and on an overcast day she turned her back to Sue and sent her away. As Lakota lay quietly with her friend, Sandy, the sky darkened and hail thundered upon the ground. As the storm raged, Sue kept hearing the words Lakota said over and over. The earth shook and Lakota was gone.

In spirit, I share my bed with humans and animals.
There is no competition, no hatred.
It is the true garden of love.
This is our desire for the earth at this time,
to re-establish this harmony among all.

Can you tell me what it is like when you pass into spirit?

"Passing out of a physical body is a surrendering to the great hands of light. When our spirit begins to lift from the body, many try to hold on, but when it is time, there is nothing that can be done except to surrender to this great force. It is powerful and fast, dizzying to some as you shift into a spiritual realm. Then you begin to feel the immense love infused over you, as if you are weak and limp, yet full of a vibration of love, like no other. You are helpless to this power, yet all trusting. You are instantly humbled and infantile, birthing into a new plane of existence. Patient and pure, you transition into an incredible brightness. Although the light is bright, it does not hurt your eyes. You feel yourself once again and know that you are no longer in the old body. You have a desire to see more and once you do they all come into view."

What comes into view?

"Whatever or whomever is waiting for you there. Your angels help you from the body. I know this because I have seen their wings. I have felt hands supporting me as I left my physical body. When you get to the light, the faces of those you have known before come into view. It is like a birth. They are excited to see you, yet you feel somehow infantile until you get accustomed to this new world. It is truly glorious, but some take longer than others to comprehend the full extent of where they are and who they are with."

"Sometimes the attachment to the physical plane inhibits the speed of the transition on the 'God' plane. Once we have fully gone through this transition, we understand on a very deep level that which we have learned and taught on a soul level on the earth plane. This is also when we assign ourselves a continuing educational course for the growth of the soul. We move within our soul family so we are always supported with love and with light. The only time we are ever alone is when we have lost the connection with our 'God' love.

But we are truly never alone. Once we are in touch with this love we see how connected we all truly are. When you are in spirit this is vitally true. I think the human race should experience being in spirit while still in body. This would be the ultimate quick fix to the physical world. Sadly, they forget. Just a minute of time in spirit would be enough to get in touch again with the understanding of divine love and the connection with all. I share my bed with humans and animals here. There is no competition, no hatred. It is the true garden of love. This is our deepest desire for the earth at this time, to reestablish this harmony amongst all."

Untamed Voices is available at

www.untamedvoices.com *or on **Amazon.com***

I will always stand tall and full of might,
because I know truly who I am.
I am part of the beating heart of earth.
I have a
right to be here.

10

MAKING A DIFFERENCE

We can make a difference. Many people become overwhelmed at the amount of suffering animals endure and feel they can't do enough to help or make a difference. Each act of kindness has a ripple effect that will continue to affect change. Don't feel like you have to do it all, pick something that resonates with you and allow your heart and soul to illuminate the darkness in its own unique way.

What can you do?

Here are a few ideas:

- Spay and neuter your animals.

- Educate your children, students, community and friends as to the proper treatment of animals.

- Foster an animal.

- Sponsor an animal for a year.

- Write letters to companies engaging in animal testing, government officials, and newspapers.

- Buy cruelty free products.

- Don't buy animals from pet stores or puppy mills; adopt an animal from a shelter, rescue or sanctuary.

- Volunteer your time or expertise at a local animal sanctuary or shelter.

- Ask what the shelters in your area need and create a supply drive or donate items.

- Do not buy fur.

- Make conscious food choices:

- Consider going vegetarian or vegan one or more days a week.
- Choose free-range or organic foods.
- Avoid food from factory farms.

- Pick up trash and recycle.

- Choose environmentally friendly alternatives to everyday things.

- Reduce waste, conserve energy and water.

What some animals go through is inexcusable, and many times we are driven into rage. However, in order to effectively make a difference, we have to turn it around to make a positive change.

Do not advocate violence against violence, instead send love to the animals that are being unfairly treated and use your strengths to bring about change. If you are a good speaker use your voice to help; if you have effective writing or marketing skills, use your creativity to make people aware of what is going on. By throwing anger at a bad situation you are only giving it energy. Hate fuels hate. If you really want to make a change, use positive energy and you will see positive results.

The world is a place where every soul has a chance to make a difference. It is the theatre of life.

Exercise:

Practice noticing the little things in life that are so special. The smell of coffee in the morning, the way the sun sets over the trees, the sound of the birds calling to each other, and the way the sun hits the petal of a flower. Pay attention to the little details and give thanks for being able to experience it on a level beyond simply viewing. You can keep a gratitude journal if you like or just give thanks during the day for each experience.

Exercise:

Create a gratitude board. Fill it with pictures of things you love, are grateful for and inspire you. You can also place sayings on the board that resonate with you and how you want to live. Have fun with it. It can be an ongoing creation and something that just makes you feel good.

Exercise:

Donate your time to a local animal shelter, rescue or sanctuary. Sit with an animal and allow them to release any fears or pain they may be carrying. Acknowledge whatever it is they need you to know. Listen without judgment and share the common language of love.

"No matter what you encounter in this life, you will always have your spirit. When you forget that, you will be finished."

11

KEY POINTS

✓ Telepathy is the direct transmission of feelings, intentions, thoughts, mental images, emotions, impressions, sensations and pure knowing. Telepathy means "feeling across a distance." Telepathic communication can be done in person or over distance.

✓ Humans are born with this ability, but as we are socialized we become dependent on verbal communication and our telepathic skills lay hidden. Telepathy is like a muscle, unless used regularly it becomes weak and inefficient. This is why practice is so important.

✓ The only thing that limits us.....is what our mind "thinks" we can't do!

✓ Animals are very sensitive in ways humans may not be able to relate to. Their own senses can be much more intense than we realize.

✓ When you talk to your animal, you are unconsciously sending them pictures, feelings and emotions behind the words. Animals rely heavily on this. I have found that by consciously wording things to your animal in such a way that you send a positive picture to them – positive results can be achieved.

✓ The challenge of telepathic communication is not being able to do it, we are doing it all the time without realizing it. The challenge is to access it with full awareness, attention, and trust.

✓ "Hear" not with your ears, but with reverence and respect for all beings. Remember not to judge or assume.

✓ Example of not being "grounded" is the feeling of being lightheaded or spacey after any psychic activity, meditation, or even after dreaming. If you are working with animals that may have an emotional or physical trauma that you pick up, you may inadvertently carry that emotional or physical feeling with you after you have disconnected from the animal. If this happens, you will need to ground and protect your energy.

✓ It is important that you get in the habit of protecting your energy after any type of psychic or intuitive work. I am sure you can think of instances where a certain person or place left you drained, or physically ill in some way. People have a lot of negativity and this can leach onto you and drain you of your vital energy and positivity, if you don't recognize it. They may not even be aware they are doing this. Don't worry though, you can take simple steps to keep yourself protected and continue your positive flow of energy.

✓ All things have energy. Energy is something that never dies, it just shifts and changes. Trees are alive; they have energy and access to knowledge from higher planes. Yes, we can communicate with trees, plants, flowers, insects, fish, etc.

✓ The importance of sending information to an animal clearly is often overlooked. By being present in the moment and clear in your messages, you increase your accuracy that the animal will understand and that you will receive information clearly as well.

✓ By setting your intention to connect with a certain animal you are setting up a direct transmission to that animal. Just like a radio, if you have a poor connection there may be a lot of static to pick through. If our mind is full of other thoughts when you connect with an animal, the connection will not be as pure as it could be. Keep things simple and clear in the beginning.

✓ Keep your pictures and words crisp and clear. When you are picturing something for an animal, create the scene as realistic as possible.

✓ Animals want to know what "to do," not what "not" to do. They often read the pictures behind our words. By telling an animal what we want them to do, we send a picture of exactly that.

✓ Stating your intention during a long distance communication is a very important step. This sets up the connection to the exact animal you wish to connect with. It is like plugging into their energy.

✓ The way you view animals will influence your communication receptivity and the willingness of the animals you are connecting with. Approach animals with respect and appreciation for who they are. If you view them as substandard or inferior in any way, you will limit your ability and awareness. In order to truly experience the spiritual essence of each being you will need to leave any preconceived notions and fears behind. Open your heart, and allow the animal's true being to come through to you. Be humble and receptive and the animals will feel comfortable opening up to you.

✓ Telepathy is a wonderful tool to help your animals communicate to you the areas on their body that hurt or are a concern.

✓ You can do a body scan a few different ways:

Imagine your energy overlapping into the body of an animal, watching the animal move in your mind's eye and moving through the body like a laser beam.

✓ The sensations will be subtle. For instance, you may get a quick ache in your ankle, your shoulder blade may feel itchy, or you may feel your attention going to your stomach all of a sudden.

✓ See it, feel it, sense it. You can get health information in a variety of ways. Make sure you write down whatever you get in any form you get it.

✓ Remember, describe what you get – don't diagnose.

✓ Animals, like people, heal on different levels. Sometimes a physical problem is caused by an emotional upset that happened years ago. And, unless the animal heals the emotional aspect of the illness, the physical manifestation may not respond well to treatment.

✓ Certain things must be present within yourself to access telepathy successfully such as love, trust, and honor for yourself and others.

✓ No one person can access all the information at once. We receive messages in a variety of different ways. Think of it as a big ball of energy that we "translate and interpret." We pull from it what we can, but not necessarily all of it. Each person may interpret a different part of that ball of energy, yet arrive at the same conclusion.

✓ Distinguishing between your logical mind and the energy of the animal is the ongoing challenge of telepathic communication. The more you "do it" the more confidence you will have in trusting that you are connecting with an animal.

✓ Put your own fears, beliefs and baggage aside. When another being is speaking we must practice being present and listening.

✓ In order for you to continue to advance with any type of spiritual work, such as animal communication, you should take time to keep your body, mind, and spirit as balanced as possible.

✓ Ask the animal to give you a sign when they need help passing over. Sometimes you will just know in your heart it is time.

✓ Communication with different species will help to develop your telepathic muscle as well as a spiritual reverence for all living things.

✓ Give your animal permission to leave their body. It is important that you not just say this, but also mean it from your heart. Allow your animal to make the journey with all the love in your heart.

✓ Animals will often visit us in dreams after they have passed. It is the easiest way for them to communicate with us from spirit. Many times they visit just to let us know they are okay.

✓ Death is a transition out of the physical body, it is a freeing of the spirit.

✓ Some animals leave this life it seems well before their time. It may be because they only have a short contract here on earth, or they feel that they have completed their purpose here. Sometimes an animal's death is a part of our growth. Animals sometimes leave to make room for another or to be on the other side to help a friend that has passed or will be passing.

✓ There is a reason for everything; unfortunately, the big picture may not unfold completely for us until we are reunited on the other side.

✓ When an animal passes they cross a rainbow bridge to the other side that is so full of vibrant colors, beautiful sounds and loving friends that it is pure joy. We can cross this bridge anytime in our mind or through our dreams to visit our animal friends. When our time comes, they will be there to greet us upon our arrival.

Animals teach us how to play and live in the moment, they teach us respect, humility, patience, joy, and above all else, LOVE.

"Cats make people stop and give love. We tell them to sit still, to bend down, to reach over and to stroke our gorgeous coat. They are then allowed to give and receive love from one of the most beautiful sources in the world, a cat."

ABOUT THE AUTHOR

Debbie McGillivray is a professional animal communicator and pet intuitive with over 17 years experience and clients across the globe. She is coauthor of the book "Untamed Voices" and "The Complete Idiot's Guide to Pet Psychic Communication." Debbie believes that we all hold the ability to communicate with our animal friends and is dedicated to opening people's hearts and minds to this phenomenon. She holds workshops nationally as well as online home study courses to help people develop this ability. You can find out more about Debbie and her work at ***www.Animaltelepathy.com***.

"I feel very blessed to be able to bridge the gap between humans and animals, to bring about healing, understanding, and growth. It is through this subtle communication that

questions are answered, compromise is achieved and harmony restored. Animals have so much to teach us, all we have to do is open our hearts and listen. It is my goal and vision for people and animals to understand each other on a deeper level through mutual respect, communication, and compassion, so that we may once again live in harmony with all living things. Only then will this world be truly healed."

- Debbie McGillivray

If you listen to the animals, they will speak....

Some information in this book has been sourced by:

Untamed Voices - *2012*
Debbie McGillivray and Sue Steffens

The Complete Idiot's Guide to Pet Psychic Communication
Debbie McGillivray and Eve Adamson Copyright ©
2004 by Amaranth Illuminare

Code of Ethics for Animal Communicators
1990 – Penelope Smith

Made in the USA
Columbia, SC
27 December 2020